Why Do You Believe That?

A Protestant-Catholic Conversation

John Schwarz

with Dwight Longenecker

WHY DO YOU BELIEVE THAT? © copyright 2005 by John Schwarz. All rights reserved. No part of this book may be reproduced in any form whatsoever, by photography or xerography, or by any other means, by broadcast or transmission, by translation into any kind of language, nor by recording electronically or otherwise, without permission in writing from the author, except by a reviewer, who may quote brief passages in critical articles or reviews.

ISBN 10: 1-59298-128-3
ISBN 13: 978-1-59298-128-1

Library of Congress Catalog Number: 2005935051

Book design and typesetting: Mori Studio, Inc.
Cover design: Jaana Bykonich of Mori Studio, Inc.

Printed in the United States of America

First Printing: October 2005

08 07 06 05   6 5 4 3 2 1

Beaver's Pond Press, Inc.

7104 Ohms Lane, Suite 216
Edina, MN 55439
(952) 829-8818
www.BeaversPondPress.com

To order, visit www.BookHouseFulfillment.com or call 1-800-901-3480. Reseller and special sales discounts available.

This book is dedicated to my son, Jay Schwarz, who died in March 2005. Jay grew up Protestant and later converted to Catholicism. He suggested this book so that he and his father would better understand each other's faith and beliefs.

> *"A wise son brings joy to his father."*
> —**Proverbs 10:1**

This book is dedicated to Daryl Longenecker, the first of three brothers to enter into full communion with the Catholic Church.

> *"How good and pleasant it is when brothers dwell together in unity."*
> —**Psalm 133:1**

Table of Contents

PREFACE   ix

CHAPTER ONE: THE CHRISTIAN CHURCH
THE BIRTH, GROWTH AND TRIUMPH OF CHRISTIANITY   1
- The Founding of Christianity: "He is Risen. Yes, Risen Indeed!"   1
- The Outward Movement: From Jerusalem to Rome   3
- The Post-Apostolic Church: Presbyters, Bishops, Canon and Creeds   4
- The Middle Ages: The Rise of Papal Power and Authority   8
- The East-West Schism: Roman Catholicism and Eastern Orthodoxy   10

CHAPTER TWO: THREE STRIKES AND YOU'RE OUT
THE PROTESTANT REFORMATION   15
- The Underlying Causes of the Reformation   15
- Martin Luther: The Father of the Protestant Reformation   18
- John Calvin: The Architect of Reformed Protestantism   21
- Reformation Theology: The Word Alone, Faith Alone and Christ Alone   22

- The Reformations: Lutheran, Reformed, Anglican and Radical   23
- The Council of Trent: The Catholic Counter-Reformation   26

CHAPTER THREE: ALL IN FAVOR
SHARED PROTESTANT-CATHOLIC BELIEFS   29
- The Scriptures: Revelation, Inspiration and Authority   31
- God the Father: The Knowledge, Trinity and Attributes of God   33
- Humankind: Children of God and Heirs of Adam and Eve   35
- Jesus Christ: The Incarnate Son of God   37
- Salvation: By Grace, Through Faith   39
- The Holy Spirit: Gifts, Regeneration and Sanctification   40
- The Church: One, Holy, Universal and Apostolic   41
- The End Times: Resurrection, Intermediate State and Eternity   43

CHAPTER FOUR: NEVER THE TWAIN SHALL MEET
SOLA SCRIPTURA* AND *SOLA FIDE   45
- The Basis of Authority: The Word of God   45
  - Protestantism: *Sola Scriptura*   47
  - Catholicism: Scripture and Tradition   51
  - The Magisterium   54
- The Means and Assurance of Salvation   56
  - Protestantism: *Sola Fide*   57
  - Catholicism: Faith, Sacraments and Works   57
  - The Assurance of Salvation   60

CHAPTER FIVE: PETER, PAUL AND MARY
THE PAPACY AND THE VIRGIN MARY   63
- The Pope: Christ's Vicar on Earth   63
  - Apostolic Succession: From the First Century to the Twenty-first   68
  - Papal Infallibility: Without Error   70

- Mary: The Mother of God   72
  - Mary's Sinlessness: The Immaculate Conception   74
  - Mary's Perpetual Virginity: Before, During and After   76
  - Mary's Assumption into Heaven: At the Right Hand of Jesus   79

CHAPTER SIX: THE SACRAMENTS
MYSTERY, MEANING AND MUMBO JUMBO   83
- The Sacraments: Means of Grace or Symbols of Grace?   83
- The Gospel Sacraments   84
  - Baptism: "In the Name of the Father, the Son and the Holy Spirit"   85
  - Holy Communion/Eucharist: "Do This in Remembrance of Me"   87
- The Tridentine Sacraments   93
  - Confirmation: Affirmation and Sealing of the Holy Spirit   93
  - Reconciliation: Confession, Penance and Absolution   95
  - Matrimony: "And the Two Shall Become One Flesh"   97
  - Holy Orders: The Consecration of Those Called to Ministry   99
  - Anointing the Sick: Prayers of Healing and Preparation for Death   103

CHAPTER SEVEN: UNIQUE CATHOLIC BELIEFS
STANDARD EQUIPMENT OR OPTIONAL EXTRAS?   107
- Catholic Sacramentals: The Rosary, Water, Genuflection and More   107
- Canonicity: The Catholic Old Testament   110
- Purgatory: The Intermediate State   113
- The Saints: Beatification, Canonization and Veneration   116

SOME FINAL THOUGHTS   119

A GUIDE TO FURTHER READING   125

INDEX OF NAMES   139

ABOUT THE AUTHORS   143

Preface

The idea for this book came from Jay Schwarz, who converted to Catholicism in his early 20s and spent ten years in a Catholic order. Jay had read *Letters from a Skeptic*, a book of letters exchanged between a skeptical Catholic father and his Protestant son, Greg Boyd, who at the time was professor of religion at Bethel University in St. Paul, Minnesota. Jay said to his father, John, "We should do a book like the Boyds, with questions from a Protestant father to his Catholic son about Catholicism." Jay and John did a lot of work on the book, and were still discussing it back and forth when Jay died unexpectedly of a heart attack in March 2005. At the time of his death, Jay was an adjunct professor and doctoral student at the University of Dallas, 'The Catholic University for Independent Thinkers.'

Why Do You Believe That? is an easy-to-read primer for lay Catholics and Protestants on the church's rise to prominence in the years following Jesus' death and resurrection; the Protestant Reformation in the sixteenth century, which split the Western Church into Catholic and Protestant; the many beliefs that Protestants and Catholics share in common; and, where there are differences, the underlying historical and scriptural reasons for the differences.

John Schwarz is an evangelical Protestant and writes from this perspective. To be 'fair and balanced,' John asked Catholic author and writer Dwight Longenecker to respond to questions that Protestants have about Catholicism in the hope of bringing Catholics and Protestants closer together. The following is a brief introduction to John and Dwight; there is more information about them in the last section of the book, entitled 'About the Authors.'

John: I grew up in a Minneapolis suburb that was predominantly Protestant. I was raised in the Episcopal Church, where I was an acolyte as a young boy and later confirmed. I don't remember more than one or two friends or classmates who were Catholic. When I graduated from middle school I went to high school in Minneapolis, because my suburb did not have a high school. There I met lots of Catholics. I didn't know what they believed. I knew a few Lutherans, and some Presbyterians and Methodists; they believed many of the same things I did, or so I thought. Catholics were different. They couldn't eat meat on Friday; many wore chains with crosses around their necks; they talked about having to go to confession and catechism classes and not missing Mass; and when playing sports, they often crossed themselves before shooting a free throw or when they came up to bat in a baseball game.

One Sunday I went to church with a Catholic friend and found myself in a completely new environment. When people entered the church, they put their fingers in a font and made the sign of the cross, some lit little candles, most genuflected before sitting down, and many took rosaries out of their pockets, none of which I had ever seen before. The liturgy was in Latin, so I didn't understand much, and I wondered if my friend did because he didn't know any Latin either. When the celebrating priest elevated the host, bells rang. We didn't ring bells in the Episcopal Church. And when the Eucharist was served at the communion rail, which I had taken many times in my Episcopal church, I was told to stay in my seat because I was not Catholic.

Preface

I thought the Lord's Supper was for all *baptized Christians*. During the prayer period, prayers were offered for the Pope, who during those years was Pope Pius XII, and also to Mary. Episcopalians didn't pray for the Archbishop of Canterbury, the leader of the worldwide Anglican Communion, nor to Mary. As you can see, there was much about Catholicism I didn't understand, and this was true of most of my Protestant friends, and still is today. It is my hope that this book will help Protestants and Catholics better understand one another.

Dwight: I was brought up in a conservative evangelical home in Pennsylvania. My dad was a deacon in a local independent Bible church. My awareness of Catholics was much like John's. In Pennsylvania we divided pretty much along ethnic and religious lines. Those of German and English descent tended to be Protestant; those of Irish, Polish and Italian descent were mostly Catholic. My first experience of Catholic worship was attending the wedding of one of my grade school teachers. My main memory was of the kneelers in the church and ladies wearing lacy head coverings.

After high school I went to Bob Jones University in South Carolina. After completing my degree, I studied at Wycliffe Hall, an evangelical Anglican seminary in Oxford, England, following which I was ordained a priest in the Church of England. I served for ten years in the Anglican Church before entering into full communion in the Catholic Church. I gained an enormous amount from my evangelical upbringing and never considered my subsequent path through Anglicanism to Catholicism to be a rejection of that marvelous Christian foundation. Instead, I regard it as an addition to all the great truths of my Bible church background. My spiritual journey has been a search for the authentic, ancient, apostolic church. This is what first led me into Anglicanism. I wanted to be part of the historic stream of Christianity, which stretched right back to

Christ himself. It was this desire that finally led me and my family into the Catholic Church.

In a more personal sense, it was also the awareness that I couldn't 'do church' on my own or with my own little group of believers. I didn't want to choose the church; I wanted the church to choose me. It was a move away from church shopping to the 'old big one,' which, for all its strengths and weaknesses, is the Catholic Church.

The first two chapters in this book recap the early history of the church: how it became the dominant institution it is today, with 2 billion adherents, and how it later split into three separate branches or expressions, Roman Catholic, Eastern Orthodox and Protestant. Chapter 3 sets forth beliefs that Protestants and Catholics share in common. The final four chapters are a dialogue between John and Dwight. Chapter 4 discusses two bottom-line differences between Protestants and Catholics: *sola scriptura*, the Protestant belief that the Bible is the sole source of authority in matters of belief and practice; and *sola fide*, the Protestant belief in salvation by faith *alone*. Chapters 5, 6 and 7 have to do with the papacy, Mary, the sacraments, purgatory and other Catholic beliefs. A brief summary of the book is as follows.

Chapter One tells the story of the church in the years following Jesus' death and resurrection: how it began, grew and became the dominant institution in Western Europe following the fall of Rome. It also tells the stories of the rise of the papacy and the Rome-Constantinople schism in the year 1054, which divided the church into Roman Catholic and Eastern Orthodox. This chapter will be helpful to those who know little about the rise of the Catholic Church, which today has some 1.1 billion baptized members.

Chapter Two tells the story of the Protestant Reformation, which was ignited when Martin Luther nailed his famous Ninety-five Theses on the door of the Castle Church in Wittenberg, Germany, in 1517, dividing the Western Church into Catholic and Protestant.

Preface

This chapter will be helpful to those who know little about the 'protests' that led to the Reformation and the various forms and expressions that Protestant Christianity has taken over the past five centuries.

Chapter Three is a mini-catechism that sets forth basic beliefs that Protestants and Catholics share in common. Traditional Catholics and evangelical Protestants both believe in the omnipotence of God, the fallen nature of humankind, Jesus' full divinity and salvific death, and in a further, fuller life to come. Evangelical Protestantism has more in common with historic Catholicism than it does with 'moderate' Protestantism, which arose in the aftermath of the Enlightenment. Moderate Protestants question the inspiration of scripture, are ambivalent about Jesus' virgin birth and miracles, reject Jesus' substitutionary death, and have trouble believing that Jesus rose bodily from the grave on Easter morning.

Chapter Four is a discussion of long-standing divisions between Protestants and Catholics having to do with the source of authority and the means of salvation. Most Protestants believe that the Bible is the sole source of authority in matters of faith and practice. Catholics also believe in the authority of scripture, but give equal weight to church-based tradition. The second principal difference has to do with salvation. Protestants believe that salvation is by grace alone through faith alone. Catholics also believe in grace and faith, but faith, to be *saving* faith, must be accompanied by observance of the sacraments and doings works of charity.

Chapters Five, Six and Seven are a dialogue between the two authors about Catholic beliefs and practices relating to the office and authority of the papacy; Mary's immaculate conception, perpetual virginity and bodily assumption; the sacraments and Catholic sacramentals; and canonicity, purgatory and the veneration of saints.

This book has several unique features. First, most Catholic-Protestant books do not tell the reader how the church became the dominant institution it is today and the reasons for its division into three separate traditions, Catholic, Orthodox and Protestant. The background information in Chapters 1 and 2 will help readers understand the two 'schisms' that divided the church into these three streams or traditions. Second, most books on Catholicism and Protestantism fail to mention that Catholics and Protestants share many common beliefs, as summarized in Chapter 3. Such books tend to focus, instead, on Catholic-Protestant differences and are often written from a polemical point of view. Third, most Protestant books on Catholicism do not allow for Catholic answers to Protestant questions about Catholic beliefs and practices. An important feature of this book is the dialogue between John and Dwight, which appears throughout the book, most notably in Chapters 4, 5, 6 and 7. It also allows for Catholic questions about Protestantism, which one rarely sees in books of this nature.

We want to acknowledge and thank the following people for reviewing, commenting on and correcting this book. On the Protestant side: Roy A. Harrisville Jr., ThD, professor emeritus, Luther Seminary (St. Paul); Ward W. Gasque, PhD, president emeritus, Pacific Association for Theological Studies (Seattle); and Grayson J. Carter, PhD, associate professor of church history, Fuller Theological Seminary Southwest (Phoenix). On the Catholic side: Christopher J. Malloy, PhD, assistant professor of theology, University of Dallas; Rev. J. Michael Byron, STD, assistant professor of systematic theology, The Saint Paul Seminary School of Divinity (St. Paul); and Christopher J. Zealley, MA, St. Philip's Books (Oxford, England). The book that you have in your hand reflects the thinking of those above, though not necessarily the complete and total view of any one of them individually.

The version of the Bible used for Scripture quotations is the *New Revised Standard Version*, copyright 1989 by the Division of Christian Education of the National Council of Churches of Christ in the USA. In certain instances, words quoted in Bible passages have been italicized for emphasis.

ONE

The Christian Church

The Birth, Growth and Triumph of Christianity

According to the *World Christian Encyclopedia* (2001), the most authoritative source of statistical information on religious belief systems, Christianity is far and away the largest religion in the world. In the year 2000, there were 2 billion Christians, representing one-third of the world's population; by the year 2050, Christianity is projected to grow by 53 percent to slightly more than 3 billion. The year 2000 numbers for the other major world religions are as follows: Islam, 1.2 billion; Hinduism, 810 million; Buddhism, 360 million; and Judaism, 14 million.

THE FOUNDING OF CHRISTIANITY
"He is Risen! Yes, Risen Indeed!"

There were many Jewish messianic movements before and after Jesus. When a leader died or was killed, his followers either found another messiah to follow or the movement collapsed. Why did the 'Jesus movement' survive—not only survive, but *flourish*, with large, thriving, racially-diverse communities of believers all over the Mediterranean world? The reason was that Jesus' followers were convinced that he had risen from the dead, and that those who believed in him would also be raised. What convinced Jesus' followers that he had been raised and was now, again, alive?

First, the empty tomb. If the Jewish leaders had wished to dispute the disciples' claim that Christ had risen from the dead, they would have needed only to go to the family tomb of Joseph of Arimathea and produce Jesus' body. This would have put an end to everything. The German theologian Paul Althaus said, "The claim that Jesus had been raised could not have been maintained for a single day, or a single hour, if the emptiness of the tomb had not been established as a fact for all concerned."

Second, the witness of Jesus' disciples. When Jesus died, his disciples went into hiding, fearing that Jesus' fate might also be theirs. Fifty days later, on the first Christian Pentecost, they began preaching on the streets of Jerusalem, and later throughout the Roman Empire, that Jesus had been raised from the dead—and many were martyred for doing so, both in Jerusalem, like Stephen and James, and in Rome, like Peter and Paul. Christian apologist Paul Little, in his book *Know Why You Believe*, said, "People will die for what they *believe* is true, but no one willingly dies for what they *know* is false."

Third, the New Testament accounts of Jesus' post-resurrection appearances. No one would have taken the time or gone to the expense of writing and copying manuscripts about an executed Jewish peasant from rural Galilee if he had remained in the grave. Further, in the first century, women were not considered credible witnesses, yet all four Gospels report that Jesus first appeared to "the women" (see Mark 16:1-8). If the writers had fabricated their stories to make them more credible, they would have had men, not women, as the first witnesses.

If Jesus had not been raised from the dead, how are we to explain the rise, spread and eventual triumph of Christianity? Christian writer Frederick Buechner, in his book *The Magnificent Defeat*, said, "Unless something very real took place on that strange [Easter] morning, there would be no New Testament, no Church and no

Christianity." Why not? Because a dead, still-in-the-tomb savior would not have been *good news*.

Dwight: Easter Sunday is where the three great Christian traditions unite, in opposition to those who water down or deny the Resurrection. The Eastern Orthodox bishop Kallistos Ware said, "There are now only two types of people in the world—those who believe in Jesus' bodily resurrection and those who do not." The reason I enjoy fellowship with people like you, John, is that we both believe that Jesus is the incarnate Son of God, who was raised from the dead and reigns with God and is our living, loving Lord and Savior.

THE OUTWARD MOVEMENT
From Jerusalem to Rome

Jesus' final charge and commission to his disciples in Matthew's Gospel was to take the good news to "all nations" (28:19), meaning to all peoples, and in the book of Acts "to the ends of the earth" (1:8), meaning throughout the Roman Empire. The book of Acts is the second half of Luke's two-volume work on the origins of Christianity. It opens with an account of Jesus and his disciples in Jerusalem. On the first Pentecost, a Greek word meaning *fiftieth*, because it was the fiftieth day after Passover, the Holy Spirit descended upon Jesus' followers, empowering them to go forth into the world with the message of the good news. Just as the Spirit came upon Jesus at his baptism, which launched him on his mission to Israel, so the Spirit came upon his followers at Pentecost, which launched them on their mission to the ends of the earth.

In the years immediately following Jesus' death, resurrection and ascension, Jewish Christians—Jews who believed that Jesus was the promised Messiah—were forced out of the synagogues in Jerusalem, and over time out of Jerusalem as well. This moved the center of Christianity from Jerusalem, the center of the Judeo-Christian world, to Rome, the center of the socio-political world. The Jewish persecution of Christians did not weaken or enfeeble the Jesus movement; rather, it disbursed it far and wide, resulting in the proclamation of the good news throughout the Roman Empire.

The Post-Apostolic Church
Presbyters, Bishops, Canon and Creeds

As the Christian Church took shape, three things were necessary to assure its survival. First, it needed an effective organizational structure; second, it needed an agreed-upon canon of scripture; third, it needed to define and articulate its central beliefs in concise, concrete, creedal form.

Structure and Organization. This book is about Catholicism and Protestantism, the two largest expressions of Christianity, which we tend to identify as the Western Church, because Europe is the cradle out of which Christianity grew and spread to the rest of the world. The church, however, started in the East—in cities like Antioch, Constantinople and Alexandria. Furthermore, the debates which framed the church's thinking regarding the Trinity and the person and nature of Christ took place at councils at Nicea, Constantinople, Ephesus and Chalcedon, cities in what is today Turkey in Asia Minor. These councils formulated the basic doctrines of Christianity, which we profess to this day.

The early churches were led by *presbyters*, a term derived from a Greek word meaning 'elder,' from which we also get the word 'priest.' We see the emergence of church leaders in the New Testament, with Paul appointing Timothy and Titus as church leaders in Ephesus and Crete, and Peter giving advice to those in leadership positions in churches he apparently oversaw in Asia Minor and Europe (1 Peter 1:1). As the church grew, senior presbyters were appointed to oversee churches within ecclesiastical *dioceses*, a Greek term for administrative units within the Roman Empire. Senior presbyters were later called *bishops*, from the Latin translation of the Greek word *episkopos*, meaning 'overseer' or 'supervisor.'

Bishops were charged with the responsibility of safeguarding the testimony and witness of the early apostles, administering churches within their dioceses, settling disputes and quarrels between churches, and representing their dioceses at church-wide councils. During the early centuries, bishops were chosen by their communities and confirmed by neighboring bishops. (Ambrose was made bishop of Milan in 373 by public acclamation.) Gradually, the selection of bishops was turned over to existing bishops. Today the selection of bishops is the exclusive right of the bishop of Rome, the pope, to whom all bishops are answerable.

THE NEW TESTAMENT CANON. To assure the faithful transmission of the apostolic message, the church recognized certain writings as authoritative. The basis on which books were admitted to the *canon*—a Greek word meaning measuring rod or rule—was threefold. First, the authors had to have had apostolic credentials, or a close association with an apostle, as Mark had with Peter and Luke had with Paul. Second, the books had to be consistent with the church's teachings regarding the life, death and resurrection of Jesus. Third, the books had to have enjoyed church-wide acceptance and usage.

As early as the middle of the second century, there was agreement on twenty of the twenty-seven books in the New Testament—all except Hebrews, an anonymous book originally thought to have been written by the apostle Paul; the letters of James, 2 Peter, 2 and 3 John and Jude; and the book of Revelation. Official confirmation of the books in the New Testament occurred at the Synod of Carthage in 397, though final agreement on the twenty-seven books probably occurred in the mid-third century. According to British scholar John A. T. Robinson, in his book *Can We Trust the New Testament?*, "The wealth of manuscripts [more than 5,000 manuscripts have been discovered], and the narrow interval of time between the writing and the earliest extant copies, make [the New Testament] by far the best-attested text of any writing in the ancient world."

Dwight: I'm glad you pointed out that it was the church that agreed upon and confirmed the books that made their way into the canon. We'll come back to this later, but I'd like to remind our readers that the scriptures on which Protestants base their authority gained *their* authority from the pre-existing authority of the church. Let's leave this conversation for now, but don't you agree that it's one we'll have to return to?

John: Absolutely. One of the great divides between Protestantism and Catholicism is the basis of authority, which for Protestants is summarized by the term *sola scriptura*—'the scriptures alone.' We will look at this in Chapter 4. What I want to say in response to your comment about authority, Dwight, is that we see this a bit differently. First, the authority of the Bible comes from its God-given inspiration. Second, as to which came first, Protestants agree that communities of Christians existed prior to the writing of the New Testament, but insist that it was the apostolic witness and resultant writings that gave rise to these communities, not the other way around. The scriptures did not gain their authority *from* the church; rather, the church *affirmed* the authority which the scriptures already—that is, inherently—possessed.

THE APOSTLES' AND NICENE CREEDS. The third ingredient in the development of the early church was the need for creedal statements to assure the faithful witness and transmission of the apostolic message. The great theological and christological debates having to do with the triune nature of God and the person and saving work of Jesus took place at church-wide councils at Nicea in 325, Constantinople in 381, Ephesus in 431 and Chalcedon in 451.

The creeds—from the Latin *credo*, meaning 'I believe'—are drawn from scripture and take much of their support from scripture; they are, it is said, scripture in 'short hand.' The Apostles' Creed evolved from several prior creeds, including an early baptismal creed. The first mention of an *apostles* creed occurred in the year 390. Its name comes from a legend that each of the apostles contributed a clause or an article to the creed before departing on their respective missions (the original form of the creed had twelve 'clauses'). The Apostles' Creed is used only in the Western Churches; the Eastern Orthodox Church uses the Nicene Creed.

In the year 325, Emperor Constantine convened a council of bishops at Nicea, a city close to Constantinople, to resolve a dispute regarding the *person* of Jesus. Some 250 bishops attended the council, almost all of whom came from churches in the East. The council was called to settle the question of Jesus' divinity: was he fully and truly God, or less than God, since he was begotten of the Father and thus *created*? The Council of Nicea declared that Jesus was "very God of very God, begotten not made, of one substance with the Father." The Nicene Creed was expanded and made more precise at the Council of Constantinople in 381. It is the most universal of the creeds, accepted by Roman Catholics, Protestants and the Eastern Orthodox. It is sometimes said that the Nicene Creed, the Ten Commandments, the seven sacraments and the Lord's Prayer are the four foundational pillars of Catholicism.

In the fifth century, another dispute arose regarding the *nature* of Christ. Was Jesus part-God and part-human; and if there were 'parts,' were they equal, and were they separate or mixed? In the year 451, a council was called at Chalcedon, also near Constantinople, to settle the dispute. The council declared that Jesus was *one* person with two equal 'natures,' which were neither separate nor mixed.

Dwight: There are two things that I would like to mention regarding the creeds. First, they were born out of controversy. Christians have been debating doctrinal matters for as long as there has been a church, going all the way back to the apostles, who themselves had their fair share of spats, so our dialogue is in a good tradition, John! Second, the creeds were necessary because the scriptures did not explain everything. This is something that Protestants often overlook in their *sola scriptura* theology. If the scriptures had stated everything clearly, in black and white, there would have been no need for creeds. Christians quarreled in the beginning, and still do today, and the church needed agreed-upon creeds that expressed teachings that were implicit in scripture in exact, succinct language.

The Middle Ages
The Rise of Papal Power and Authority

The Middle Ages is defined, roughly, as the period between the fall of Rome in the fifth century to the Renaissance in the fifteenth century. The Christian 'hinge' figures at either end were Augustine (354-430), the last of the great church fathers, and Martin Luther (1483-1546), the great reformer. Two big events during this period were the East-West schism (from a Latin word meaning to 'split' or 'tear') in 1054, which divided the church into Roman Catholic and Eastern Orthodox, which we will look at in the following section; and the Crusades (1095-1291), a two-hundred-year military campaign to expel the Muslims from the Holy Land. The Crusades started well but ended poorly, as the crusaders turned their attention from recapturing the holy places of Christendom to pillaging, rape and murder.

The Papal Monarchy. The Roman Empire lasted for more than twelve hundred years, from the founding of Rome in 753 BC to the fall of Rome in 476 AD. In the year 410, the Visigoths entered and sacked the city of Rome, and then left. Rome finally fell in the year 476. The fall of Rome was the fall of the Western Empire; the Eastern or Byzantium Empire continued for another thousand years, falling to the Ottoman Turks in 1453. When the Western Empire fell, the church in Rome became the dominant institution in Europe: it was the largest and most important church in Christendom; it was situated in the ancient, imperial capital of the empire; and its roots went back to Peter and Paul, whose martyred remains were buried there. It is said that Peter's bones lie beneath the altar in Saint Peter's Basilica (archaeological work in the mid-twentieth century located what is believed to have been Peter's grave, directly beneath the great altar); and that Saint Paul is buried in Saint Paul's-Outside-the-Walls at *Tre Fontane* ('Three Fountains').

Christianity became the official religion of the Roman Empire in the year 380. In the mid-400s, with the papacy of Leo the Great (papal reign: 440-461), we see the dawning of a monarchial approach to the papacy. A century and a half later, Gregory the Great (papal reign: 590-604) asserted that the bishop of Rome was the supreme pontiff of both the western and eastern churches. It was during this period that the church began addressing the bishop of Rome as the *pope*, from the Latin *papa*, meaning 'father.' Catholics also call the pope Holy Father and His Holiness.

Toward the end of the first millennium, the church became deeply involved in politics. It owned land—the Papal States in central Italy and eastern France—passed laws, judged cases and even declared war. The church joined with secular kings and princes for both protection and power, beginning in 800, when Pope Leo III crowned the Frankish king Charlemagne ('Charles the Great') the Holy Roman Emperor. This practice was discontinued in 1562.

Saint Peter's Basilica is the mother church of the Catholic Church. (A *basilica* was a large public building in ancient Rome. The early church adapted its architectural style and form for its principal churches.) The original Saint Peter's was begun during the reign of Constantine in the early fourth century. The present church was begun by Pope Julius II in 1506; it was dedicated by Pope Urban VIII in 1626. The money to build the church came, principally, from the sale of indulgences, the spark that set off the Protestant Reformation.

Monasticism. One response to the church's institutionalization was monasticism, a way of showing one's devotion to Jesus by living a life of prayer, study, meditation and fasting, and also celibacy, a sign of holiness that became normative for priests, monks and nuns in the twelfth century. Communal monasticism began in Egypt in the early 300s. Benedict of Nursia (Italy), whose followers founded the *Order of Saint Benedict* (OSB) in the 500s, is considered the 'father' of western monasticism. His rules—The Rule of Saint Benedict—regarding community life, prayer, manual labor and the study of scripture set the pattern for monastic communities of monks, from the Latin *monachos*, meaning one who lives alone.

Three important orders were founded in the latter years of the Middle Ages. The *Order of Friars Minor* (OFM), the 'Lesser Brothers,' was founded in 1209 by Francis of Assisi (north central Italy). The Franciscans were *mendicants* who depended on alms for subsistence. They ministered to the sick, the poor and the destitute. The *Dominican Order of Preachers* (OP) was founded in 1216 by Dominic of Castile (Spain). The Dominicans established universities and seminaries to educate the clergy. The greatest Dominican scholar was Thomas Aquinas who, in 1880, was made the patron saint of all Catholic schools and universities. The *Society of Jesus* (SJ), more popularly known as the *Jesuits*, was founded in 1534 by Ignatius of Loyola (Spain). The Jesuits are Catholicism's largest order, with some 25,000 priests. The Jesuits led the counterattack against the Reformation and launched the expansion of the Catholic Church into India, North and South America and the Orient.

THE EAST-WEST SCHISM
Roman Catholicism and Eastern Orthodoxy
The Christian Church had several important centers or *sees*, a term derived from a Latin word referring to the seat of a bishop or his jurisdiction. The two principal centers were Rome in the West and Constantinople in the East. Constantinople was the ancient city of Byzantium, which the Emperor Constantine renamed Constantinople—the City of Constantine—when he moved his capital from

Rome to Byzantium in 330. (In 1930 Constantinople was renamed Istanbul, now the largest city in Turkey.)

The Eastern and Western Churches were separated by *distance*: Rome and Constantinople were one thousand miles apart. By *language*: the West spoke Latin and the East spoke Greek. And by different *authorities*: in the West, the principal authority was the bishop of Rome (the pope); in the East, the principal authority was the ecumenical councils. Three important differences between the Eastern and Western Churches were as follows.

First, the Eastern Church did not accept the bishop of Rome as the reigning authority over the church. The ancient governing patriarchs of Jerusalem, Constantinople, Antioch, Alexandria and Rome were viewed as equals. Among the five, the patriarch or bishop of Rome was recognized as the 'first among equals,' because of Rome's leadership of the early church, but not the supreme authority over the whole church.

Second, the Eastern Church, following the teachings of the ecumenical councils, believed that the Holy Spirit proceeded from God the Father *through* the Son, as set forth in the Nicene Creed. The Western Church began to teach that the Spirit proceeded from the Father *and* the Son. These words were added to the Nicene Creed by the Western Church at the non-ecumenical Council of Toledo (Spain) in 589. The Eastern Church resented the fact that the Western Church added the phrase "and the Son" to the Nicene Creed without its approval.

Third, the Eastern Church venerated *icons*—paintings, frescos and mosaics—of Jesus, Mary and the saints that were used as teaching devices and for devotions. Some in the Western Church opposed icons, believing they were contrary to the commandment against the veneration of idols and images. (This controversy was resolved in favor of the East.) Furthermore, the Eastern Church used leavened bread for the Eucharist, whereas the Western Church used unleavened bread; and the Eastern clergy could marry prior to ordination, whereas the Western clergy was celibate.

The Eastern and Western Churches struggled over issues of doctrine, power and authority. Things came to a head in the year 1054 when a representative of Pope Leo IX entered the Church of Hagia Sophia ('Holy Wisdom') in Constantinople and laid a papal bull—from the Latin *bulla*, meaning 'seal,' referring to the lead seal attached to papal edicts—on the altar of the church, excommunicating Michael Cerularius, the patriarch of Constantinople, for overstepping his authority. Cerularius responded in kind and excommunicated the bishop of Rome, and the church split into Roman Catholic and Eastern Orthodox. The double excommunications were lifted by Pope Paul VI and Athenagoras I, the Ecumenical Patriarch, in 1964, but the schism continues to the present day.

The phrase *Roman Catholic* means that the Western Church owes its allegiance to Rome and that it is 'catholic,' from the Greek *katholikos*, meaning 'general' or 'universal.' The term *Orthodox* means true or correct belief, based on the pronouncements of the first seven ecumenical councils. (The Eastern Church recognizes as authoritative only the first seven councils; the Catholic Church recognizes twenty-one councils, the last being Vatican II in 1962-65; most Protestants recognize only Nicea, Constantinople, Ephesus and Chalcedon.) Efforts were made to reconcile the Western and Eastern Churches, but a tragic event put an end to this. During the Fourth Crusade (1202-1204), the crusaders, on their way to the Holy Land, passed through Constantinople and desecrated Hagia Sophia on Easter Sunday 1203 and ruthlessly sacked and plundered the city, which sealed the schism.

The Eastern Orthodox Church is a federation of self-governing national churches. Three well-known Orthodox churches are the Greek Orthodox Church, the Russian Orthodox Church and the Serbian Orthodox Church. According to the *World Christian Ency-*

clopedia, the Orthodox Church has some 215 million adherents, half of which live in the former Soviet Union. Eastern Orthodox Christians first came to the United States in 1794; today there are approximately 6 million Orthodox Christians in the U. S. The Orthodox Church has an Ecumenical Patriarch in Istanbul, who exercises a degree of influence over the Church, but has no pope-like jurisdictional authority; patriarchs in Jerusalem, Alexandria, Istanbul and other eastern cities; and both metropolitans (archbishops) and bishops. Clergypersons are male-only, who can marry before ordination but not after (it is estimated that 90 percent of all Orthodox priests are married). Orthodox bishops are chosen primarily from monastic orders, and are always celibate.

Eastern Orthodoxy is close to Roman Catholicism in its acceptance of tradition (Chapter 4), the observance of seven sacraments, episcopal (bishopric) polity, and the veneration of Mary as the God-bearer. In Orthodoxy, the sacraments are called Holy Mysteries, of which baptism and Holy Eucharist are the most important. (It is said that the Orthodox prefer the term 'mystery' because the sacramental transmission of God's grace is a mystery.) Baptism is by triple immersion, after which the baptized child or adult is anointed with oil to seal the indwelling of the Holy Spirit. The Orthodox Old Testament is the Greek *Septuagint* (Chapter 7), and its primary confession is the Nicene Creed, without the 'and the Son' clause. Orthodox worship services tend to be elaborate and express Orthodoxy's affinity for mysticism.

The Great Schism between the Western and Eastern Churches in 1054 was a tragic event, but a far more serious separation occurred in the sixteenth century when the Western Church split into Roman Catholic and Protestant. The numbers and percentages of Catholic, Protestant and Orthodox Christians in the year 2000, according to the *World Christian Encyclopedia*, are set forth below. The *WCE*'s numbers are before adjustments for unaffiliated, double-affiliated and disaffiliated persons; also, the numbers of Protestants include what the *WCE* calls 'marginal' Christians, which include Mormons, Jehovah's Witnesses, Christian Scientists, Unitarians and others.

	WORLDWIDE		UNITED STATES	
	Numbers	%	Numbers	%
Roman Catholicism	1,057,300,000	50	58,000,000	26
Protestantism	833,500,000	40	155,600,000	71
Eastern Orthodoxy	215,100,000	10	5,800,000	3

The next chapter sets forth background information on the protests that led to the Reformation; the two principal Reformers, Martin Luther and John Calvin; the various expressions of Protestantism that emerged in the aftermath of the Reformation; and the Council of Trent, the Catholic response to the Reformation. The Reformation split the Western Church almost down the middle worldwide. In the United States, Protestants outnumber Catholics by roughly three-to-one.

CHAPTER TWO

Three Strikes and You're Out

The Protestant Reformation

Although the Protestant Reformation occurred a long time ago—in 2017 we will celebrate the five hundredth anniversary of Luther's posting of his Ninety-five Theses on the door of the Castle Church in Wittenberg—most Catholics and Protestants are not familiar with the *protests* that led to the Reformation, nor with the various forms and manifestations of Protestantism that were spawned by the Reformation—mainline Lutherans, Presbyterians, Methodists and Anglicans/Episcopalians; Anabaptists, Mennonites, Moravians and others, who thought that Luther and Calvin had not gone far enough; and independent Baptists, Congregationalists, Brethren and those who held that authority resided in individual congregations rather than in bishops, synods and presbyteries. Today, according to the *World Christian Encyclopedia*, there are more than 30,000 Protestant bodies or denominations, some as small as one or two churches.

THE UNDERLYING CAUSES OF THE REFORMATION

The Protestant Reformation was the second great division in the church. It split the Western Church along Northern (Germany, Switzerland, England, Scotland and Scandinavia) and Southern (Italy, France and Spain) lines, with Protestants in the majority in the Germanic north and Catholics in the Latin south. The principal protests were as follows:

First, the papal system, which concentrated ecclesiastical power and authority in the Vatican and the Roman Curia ('court'), the civil service bureaus and agencies used by the pope to administer the church.

Second, the immorality and corruption of the clergy, some of whom used their positions as avenues for personal gain. There was also widespread buying and selling of bishoprics and other clergy positions, a practice called *simony*, after Simon the sorcerer (Acts 8:18-19); and rampant nepotism, a flagrant example being that of Pope Sixtus IV (papal reign: 1471-1484), who made seven of his nephews cardinals.

Third, the Reformers taught that only two sacraments were instituted by Jesus, baptism and Holy Communion; and they rejected the teaching that observance of the sacraments was necessary for salvation, which they saw as contrary to the belief that justification or salvation comes by faith alone.

Fourth, the church's sale of indulgences for the remission of punishment for unforgiven venial sins. (Indulgences do not themselves remit sins; only the punishment due for unforgiven sins.) The proceeds from the sale of indulgences were used to finance various Vatican projects, principally the building of Saint Peter's Basilica in Rome. The Reformers saw no scriptural basis for the sale of indulgences.

Fifth, the apprehension of persons suspected of heresy, carried out by civil authorities on behalf of the church, which began in the thirteenth century and continued for several centuries thereafter. The most violent form was the Spanish Inquisition, begun by King Ferdinand and Queen Isabella in 1478, which resulted in the imprisonment and execution of thousands of alleged heretics.

Another factor in the Protestant-Catholic schism was a growth in nationalism, led by princes in Germany and elsewhere in Europe and by monarchs such as Henry VIII in England, which challenged the authority of Rome.

Dwight: Thank you for your overview of the reasons that led to the Protestant Reformation. Though we cannot discuss the reasons in detail, I want to make a few comments, and I appeal to readers on both sides of the debate to hear what the 'other side' has to say. It's amazing how different history often looks when seen from another perspective! My five comments below correspond to John's five points above.

First, it is true that the medieval Catholic Church possessed great wealth and power, but it wasn't all concentrated in Rome. Much of the church's wealth was disbursed across Europe in the form of land holdings and great abbeys and cathedrals. Also, Europe's secular princes were a constant check and balance on the power of the Vatican, in much the same way that the pope was a check and balance on the secular princes.

Second, it's true that there were elements of corruption within the corridors of power in the late fifteenth century; but it is also true that the late Middle Ages was a time of spiritual growth and passionate faith. The Catholic Church was fervent and alive and there were grassroots movements for reform all across Europe.

Third, the Catholic Church recognized seven sacramental ways that God's grace flows through the church to his people, each of which, it believed, was instituted by Jesus and supported by scripture. We will look at both the number and the different understanding of the sacraments in Chapter 6.

Fourth, Jesus gave power to his apostles to remit sins; the Catholic Church taught that this power continued in the church (Matthew 16:19). The sale of indulgences was clearly an abuse and corruption of this power, and it was right to call for its reform, which occurred a few years later at the Council of Trent.

Fifth, heresy trials did take place and suspected heretics were arrested and tortured, but, other than those of the Spanish Inquisition, these trials were more humane than most people realize and relatively few people were sent to their death.

MARTIN LUTHER
The Father of the Protestant Reformation

The German monk Martin Luther is given credit for igniting the Reformation, but the unrest that gave rise to the revolt against Rome began long before Luther arrived on the scene. John Wycliffe (1329-1384), an Oxford theologian, is called the 'Morning Star' of the Reformation. Wycliffe said that the Bible was the only authoritative guide for faith and practice (some believe that Wycliffe is responsible for the Latin phrase *sola scriptura*). Toward the end of his life, Wycliffe and his followers translated Jerome's Latin *Vulgate* into English so that it could be read by the laity. Wycliffe also spoke out against the papacy; against the belief in an unbroken line of 'apostolic succession' from the apostles to the church's bishops; and against indulgences, the 'transubstantiation' of the elements in the Eucharist and the veneration of saints.

Martin Luther was born in 1483, in the town of Eisleben in eastern Germany. He was the second and eldest surviving child of Hans Luther, a businessman who owned and operated mines and smelters. In 1505, according to legend, while a student at the University of Erfurt, Luther was caught in a violent thunderstorm near the small village of Stotternheim and knocked to the ground when a lightening bolt landed nearby. In a moment of terror he cried out to Saint Anne, the patron saint of miners, "Blessed Saint Anne! Help me and I will become a monk!" Two weeks later, to his father's great dismay, Luther honored his vow and entered the Augustinian monastery in Erfurt.

In 1507 Luther was ordained a priest; in 1512 he received a doctorate in theology; in 1513 he was appointed to the chair of biblical theology at the newly established University of Wittenberg and became the pastor of the Wittenberg's Saint Mary's Parish, a position he held until the end of his life. On October 31, 1517, Luther sent *A Disputation on the Power and Efficacy of Indulgences* to Cardinal Albrecht, the Archbishop of Mainz and Magdeburg, in whose neighboring ecclesiastical domains indulgences were being sold. (Wittenbergers were traveling to churches in Albrecht's dioceses to purchase indulgences.) Albrecht encouraged the sale of indulgences, from which he received half of the proceeds, to pay for the purchase of one of his archbishoprics.

Luther later posted the ninety-five 'theses' or propositions in the *Disputation* on the door of the Castle Church in Wittenberg, which made them readable by anyone walking past the church. The theses were not written to launch a new movement; Luther never intended to leave the Catholic Church. They were an invitation to discuss abuses that had built up over the years regarding the *sale* of indulgences, a practice that Luther saw as having no basis in scripture. Some believe that if Luther's objections had been dealt with at the outset there may have been no Reformation, but Pope Leo X needed monies from the sale of indulgences to continue the building of Saint Peter's Basilica.

Luther believed in the forgiveness of sins by and through the saving death of Christ; the Catholic Church also believed this. What Luther objected to was the payment of money to the church as pardons for unforgiven sins in the present life, and the sins of relatives and others in purgatory. The ninety-five theses were written in Latin; they were translated into German and circulated throughout the country. There was great popular support for Luther and his teachings—German Christians resented sending money from the sale of indulgences over the Alps to Rome—and great opposition to him in the Vatican.

Luther was asked to recant his views; he refused and was excommunicated (denied the sacrament of Holy Communion). In 1521, Charles V of Spain, the Holy Roman Emperor, called the Diet ('assembly') of Worms, a city in western Germany, to 'examine' Luther. Luther defended his writings against indulgences, the papacy and other matters, concluding his defense with his most remembered words: "Unless I am convinced of error by the testimony of scripture or by manifest reasoning, I cannot and will not recant anything. Here I stand. I can do no other."

Luther fell under the protection of Frederick the Wise, the 'Elector' of Saxony, one of seven princes who chose the emperors of the Holy Roman Empire. Frederick founded the University of Wittenberg in 1502. It was his pride and joy and Luther was its most important and famous professor. Following his refusal to 'recant' at Worms, Frederick's men kidnapped Luther and hid him at Frederick's Wartburg Castle (1521-1522) to prevent his arrest by Rome. During his sanctuary at Wartburg, Luther translated the New Testament into German, using Erasmus's more accurate Greek New Testament, rather than Jerome's Latin *Vulgate*; the Old Testament translation was completed in 1534. The *Luther Bible* had an enormous influence on the German language, more so even than the *King James Version* had on the English language.

In 1525 Luther married Katharina von Bora, a former Cistercian nun, whom he playfully referred to as My Rib (Martin was forty-two, Katie was twenty-six). Together they raised a family of three sons, three daughters (one died in infancy, another at age thirteen) and four orphans. Luther has been Christendom's most prolific writer, with more than five hundred published works, including long and short catechisms (instructions) on the Ten Commandments, the Apostles' Creed, the Lord's Prayer and the sacraments to teach Christian doctrine to pastors and the laity. Luther also loved music and wrote twenty-seven hymns, his most famous being *A Mighty Fortress is Our God*, often called 'The Battle

Hymn of the Reformation.' Luther died in 1546 in Eisleben, the town of his birth. Polls consistently rank him as one of the ten most important figures in the history of Western civilization, and it is said that more books have been written about Luther than any person in history, except Jesus of Nazareth.

JOHN CALVIN
The Architect of Reformed Protestantism

The other giant figure of the Reformation was the Frenchman John Calvin, who was born in 1509 in the town of Noyon, northeast of Paris. Calvin was twenty-five years Luther's junior. He was raised Catholic, but had a conversion experience in his twenties (in 1533), after which he devoted his full attention to the cause of Protestantism. Calvin was a first-class intellectual, with a renaissance education in law, humanities, philosophy, classical literature and the arts, and he was fluent in Latin, Hebrew and Greek. The center of Luther's theology was justification by faith; the center of Calvin's theology was the sovereignty of God. Calvin believed that the Bible was the only source of knowledge about God and his purposes, and the only trustworthy guide for Christian faith and practice.

Calvin spent the last twenty years of his life in French-speaking Geneva, Switzerland, where he preached and wrote commentaries on a wide range of books in both the Old and New Testaments. His most important contribution to the Reformation was the *Institutes* ('Institution') *of the Christian Religion*, which he wrote, revised and expanded four times over the years 1536 to 1559. Calvin's *Institutes* is a complete, systematic statement of Reformation theology; over time, it became the textbook for most forms of non-Lutheran Protestantism. Calvin was not as 'Catholic' as Luther and went beyond Luther's more conservative reforms regarding church polity, liturgy and the Lord's Supper. During and after Calvin's life, Geneva became the center of the non-Germanic Protestant world.

REFORMATION THEOLOGY
The Word Alone, Faith Alone and Christ Alone

The central, distinguishing differences between Reformation theology and Roman Catholicism were as follows:

First, the Reformers based their teachings solely on the Bible, a practice called *sola scriptura*—'the scriptures alone.' The Catholic Church based its teachings on both scripture and tradition, and it believed that the latter was equally authoritative with scripture.

Second, the Reformers translated the Bible into German, French, English and other languages so that it could be read by the people and thus more readily applied to their lives. The Catholic Bible was the Latin *Vulgate,* which reigned supreme in the Catholic Church until well into the twentieth century. Furthermore, the Catholic Church held itself to be the sole, official interpreter of scripture.

Third, the Reformers believed that salvation was by grace alone (*sola gratia*) through faith alone (*sola fide*). The Catholic Church also taught that salvation was by grace through faith, with one important difference: faith, to be *saving* faith, must be accompanied by observance of the sacraments and doing works of charity (Chapter 4). This was the line in the sand between the Reformers and the Catholic Church.

Fourth, the Reformers saw no scriptural basis for a priest to 'dispense' God's grace. They emphasized, instead, each person's direct access to God through Jesus, based on Paul's teaching that Jesus Christ is the only "mediator between God and humankind" (1 Timothy 2:5).

Fifth, the Reformers eliminated divisions between the clergy and the laity. The Reformers said that all Christians are called to ministry by virtue of their baptism—the 'priesthood of all believers'—not just the ordained clergy. The Catholic Church believed in a corporate priesthood, within which ordained priests exercise a unique, apostolic, God-given priestly role.

In addition, the Reformers rejected Catholic teachings regarding the papacy, indulgences and purgatory; the veneration of Mary and the saints; sacraments other than baptism and the Lord's Supper; the 'real presence' of Christ in the eucharistic bread and wine; the addition of several books to the Hebrew (Old Testament) canon; the requirement that pastors be celibate; the use of the rosary, holy water, shrines, relics (venerated physical objects) and other 'sacramentals'; and Latin as the language of the Mass.

THE REFORMATIONS
Lutheran, Reformed, Anglican and Radical

The Protestant Reformation was not a single 'reformation' but a series of reformations, which expressed itself in four principal traditions: Lutheran, Reformed and Anglican, and Radical, out of which evolved Mennonite, Brethren, Baptist, Congregational, Quaker, Methodist and other denominations.

Lutheranism was based on the writings of Martin Luther. Luther was the great champion of *sola scriptura* and justification by faith (*sola fide*), but he stayed close to the Catholic Church with regard to liturgy and church practices. He was much less 'Protestant' than the Reformers who came after him, like Ulrich Zwingli and John Calvin in Switzerland; John Knox, the father of Scottish Presbyterianism; and Thomas Cranmer, the architect of Anglican Protestantism. Luther's followers founded churches in Northern Germany, Sweden, Norway and other Scandinavian countries, and later throughout the world. The primary 'confession' of Lutheranism is the Augsburg Confession, based on Luther's writings but written and put in final form by Philip Melanchthon, Luther's most important colleague at Wittenberg. The confession, which was presented to Emperor Charles V at the Diet of Augsburg in 1530, was the earliest Protestant creedal statement.

Calvinism or **Reformed Protestantism** was more 'Protestant' than Lutheranism and became the dominant expression of Reformation theology and practice. It differed from Lutheranism with regard to church polity, with authority residing in presbyteries of pastors and elders, rather than in bishops; and in its understanding of the Lord's Supper as a spiritual union with Christ, rather than Luther's belief that Christ exists 'over, under and with' the substances (the bread and wine). Furthermore, Calvinists wanted a simple, less liturgical form of worship: no vestments, statues, stained glass windows, candles or stone altars.

The followers of Calvin founded Reformed churches on the European continent—Dutch Reformed, German Reformed, French Huguenots—and Presbyterian churches in Scotland, England and Northern Ireland. Those who came to the New World called themselves Reformed if they came from the continent and Presbyterian if they came from Great Britain and Ireland. The primary doctrinal statement of English-speaking Presbyterians is the Westminster Confession, drawn up by the Westminster Assembly in 1646, which became the creedal standard for Reformed and Presbyterian churches.

The English Reformation was less theological than political, at least at the outset. It broke communion with Rome, but did not go as far as Luther or Calvin. The English Reformation began during the reign of Henry VIII (1509-1547). Henry was married to Catherine of Aragon, the daughter of Ferdinand and Isabella of Spain. They had several children, but only Mary Tudor survived. Henry wanted a male heir to assure the survival of his dynasty. Catherine was in her forties, and the prospect of her bearing a son was not promising, so Henry had the Archbishop of Canterbury, Thomas Cranmer, annul their marriage. Shortly thereafter, Pope Clement VII excommunicated Henry. (Catherine's nephew, Charles V, the Holy Roman Emperor, was a strong ally of the pope.) In 1534 the British Parliament passed the Act of Supremacy, which made the English monarch the supreme head of the Church in England, also called the Anglican Church, from the Latin *Anglicanus*, the 'land of the Angles' or Angle-land (England). The Church of England's doctrinal statement is contained in the Thirty-nine Articles (1563), which steers a middle path between Calvinism and Catholicism. In his role as the head of the church, Henry dissolved Catholic monasteries and confiscated Catholic lands, buildings, libraries and other properties.

When Henry died in 1547, the throne passed to Edward VI, Henry's son with Jane Seymour, during whose short reign England moved in a decidedly Protestant direction. When Edward died in 1553, the throne passed to Henry and Catherine's daughter, 'Bloody Mary' Tudor, who tried to reverse the Protestant direction of England. When Mary died, five years later, Elizabeth, the daughter of Henry and Anne Boleyn, became Queen Elizabeth I. During her long reign (1558-1603), England returned to Protestantism. Today there are Anglican churches in more than 150 countries, making the Anglican Communion second only to the Catholic Church as the most widespread Christian communion. In the United States, the Anglican Church is called the Episcopal Church.

The Radical Reformation began in and around Switzerland. It consisted of a number of small, separate but related movements which advocated theological and ecclesiastical reforms more extreme than those of Luther and Calvin. Included among the radical reformers were the *Anabaptists* ('rebaptizers') in Switzerland, the forerunners of the Baptists; the *Mennonites*, founded by the Dutch Anabaptist Menno Simons, who believed in pacifism and living lives of simplicity (the *Amish* are breakaway Mennonites); the English *Puritans*, who wanted to 'purify' the state-controlled Church of England of its Romanism; the *Independents* and *Separatists*, who broke from the Church of England and came to America, where they founded independent Congregational churches; the *Baptists*, who baptized by immersion after a believer's public profession of faith, founded by John Smyth in Amsterdam; the *Society of Friends* or *Quakers*, who believed in the 'inner light' of the Spirit and that all should 'quake' before the word of God, founded by George Fox in England; and the *Methodists*, founded by followers of the Anglican brothers John and Charles Wesley, who believed that one should live according to the 'method of life' laid down in the Bible.

THE COUNCIL OF TRENT
The Catholic Counter-Reformation

When the Reformation began to spread and take root, the Catholic Church called a church-wide council at Trent in northern Italy, which met in three sessions over the years 1545-47, 1551-52 and 1562-63. The Council of Trent was the longest council in church history, and the most important Catholic council between Nicea (325) and Vatican II (1962-65). Thomas Bokenkotter, in his book *Dynamic Catholicism*, said, "Trent defined the Catholic position in such clear and trenchant language that henceforth everyone knew exactly where the Catholic Church stood."

The Council of Trent was the Catholic Church's response to the Reformation. Trent addressed issues raised by the Reformers, such as priestly morality and simony, but its primary purpose was to carefully define Catholic doctrines challenged by the Reformers. Trent affirmed and strengthened the pope's authority over the church; declared that there were seven sacraments; reaffirmed Christ's 'real presence' in the Eucharist; made the Latin *Vulgate* the official translation of the Bible; and declared that the Catholic Church was the sole, authoritative interpreter of scripture. It also condemned and abolished the sale of indulgences. The decisions and pronouncements of the Council of Trent are referred to as the *Tridentine* teachings and doctrines, derived from the Latin word *Tridentinus*, the ancient name of Trent.

In the fifteenth and sixteenth centuries, the Catholic Church began to expand beyond Europe. The great naval powers, Spain and

Portugal, were Catholic. They traveled around the globe looking for silk, spices, tea, coffee, tobacco and other items of trade, and for gold and silver. A major reason for the Catholic Church's overseas success was that it had a trained 'army' of missionaries—Jesuits, Franciscans, Dominicans and others—who accompanied the ships on their voyages (twelve priests accompanied Columbus on his second voyage in 1493). In the years following the Reformation, the Catholic Church won more converts in India, Latin America and the Orient than it lost to Protestantism within Europe.

Despite historical divisions between Catholics and Protestants, the two traditions agree on the big things—the triune nature of God; humankind's fallen nature and separation from God; the full humanity and divinity of Jesus and his saving, substitutionary death on the cross; and the final judgment and the life hereafter. The next chapter summarizes several of these shared beliefs. Protestants and Catholics are much more alike than different and need to stand together as brothers and sisters in Christ against the rising tide of militant Islam around the world.

CHAPTER THREE

All in Favor

Shared Protestant-Catholic Beliefs

Catholics and Protestants hold many beliefs in common, though the terms 'Catholic' and 'Protestant' are much too broad. Fuller Theological Seminary professor of church history Cecil Robeck, in the book *Catholics and Evangelicals*, talks about the diversity among both Catholics and Protestants. Catholicism has monastic priests and parish priests, monks and nuns, those who are cloistered and those who are not; priests who follow the Latin Rite and those who follow the Eastern Rite, whose priests are not required to be celibate; communicants who observe Holy Eucharist on a daily basis and those who do so only occasionally; those who have a deep Marian devotion and others who are primarily interested in the charismatic renewal movement. Protestantism has Presbyterian, Methodist, Episcopalian, Congregational and other mainline churches; those with strict confessions, like the Missouri Synod Lutherans and the Christian Reformed; Baptist, Brethren, Nazarene and other theologically conservative churches; Mennonites, Quakers and other 'peace' churches; and Pentecostal and African-American churches. It is not correct to talk about Catholics and Protestants as though each is a homogeneous group that believes the same thing; they do not. But there is a difference: Catholic beliefs are set forth in a clear, complete and systematic way in the *Catechism of the Catholic Church*, which applies to all

Catholics. If something is in the *Catechism*, it is official Catholic doctrine. Protestant beliefs are much more varied and eclectic, as we will see.

Dwight: I like your observations on the variety of expressions and styles within both Catholicism and Protestantism. I would be cautious, however, in confusing style with substance. Both groups might seem to have similar degrees of diversity, but there is an importance difference between the two. Baptists, Episcopalians, Presbyterians and Pentecostals, for example, have different theologies; they are not simply different in style. Furthermore, their disagreements are not about insignificant matters, like whether or not women should wear hats in church. Their differences go to questions about how a person is saved, and whether or not one can lose his or her salvation, and the meaning and efficacy of the sacraments.

Also, though there is diversity within Catholicism, most Catholics know what the Catholic Church teaches, what a sacrament is and where the source of authority lies. This is not to say that Catholics agree on every facet of the Church's teaching, as we will see later. Though they may disagree with some of the Church's teachings, or may not understand some of the Church's teachings, Catholics share a common belief that tends to unify them in a way that is quite different from Protestantism.

It may seem surprising, but evangelical Protestants have more in common with traditional, cradle-to-grave Catholics than they do with moderate Protestants, who question the inspiration and authority of scripture, the doctrines of original sin and justification by faith, and Jesus' virgin birth and bodily resurrection. The following sections are a mini-catechism of bottom-line Christian beliefs that Protestants and Catholics hold in common.

Dwight: I agree in theory that there may be a 'mere Christianity,' to use C. S. Lewis's term, to which most Christians ascribe, but it needs to be carefully defined. I hope that the conversation that follows in this and the following chapters will shed some light on this.

The Scriptures
Revelation, Inspiration and Authority

God inspired prophets and apostles to record his special revelations—the inspired word of God in the ordinary words of men. The Bible is the way that God's word continues to come to us, his 'telephone line' to us.

Revelation. God has revealed himself in and through both *general* and *special* revelation. General or Natural Revelation refers to the testimony of God in the created or natural world, a testimony to all people everywhere since the beginning of human history. Special Revelation refers to specific, progressive revelations of God: calling Abraham to leave his family and go to the land of Canaan; freeing the Israelites from their bondage in Egypt; entering into a covenant with Israel at Mount Sinai; calling prophets to exhort the Israelites to return to the covenant; coming to earth in the person of Jesus of Nazareth; sending his Spirit upon Jesus' followers on the first Pentecost; and calling Paul and others to take the good news to the "ends of the earth." The Bible is the written witness to God's *special* revelations to the patriarchs and prophets of Israel and to the apostles and followers of Jesus.

Dwight: Catholics believe in the revelation of God as recorded in scripture, but we go further. Catholics believe that tradition and the Magisterium, which we will look at more closely in the following chapter, have God-given roles in interpreting God's revelation in scripture. Unless there is a living voice—for Catholics, the church—the meaning of scripture is at the mercy of each individual or passing fashion. For Catholics, the interpretation of the Bible cannot be separated from the church.

Inspiration. The selection and superintendence of those who recorded and passed on God's word is called *inspiration*, a term which comes from a Latin word that means 'to breathe into.' The authors, though, were human and wrote for different audiences and had different sources, both oral and written (see Luke 1:1-4), which accounts for occasional differences in their stories. Some claim that every word in the Bible is inspired, a view called *verbal* inspiration, and that the Bible is *inerrant*, meaning without error in all regards, even concerning matters of history, science and geography. Those holding this position believe that admitting to the possibility of errors in the Bible is the first step down the slippery slope to unbelief. A softer view of inerrancy, called 'limited inerrancy,' maintains that the Bible is without error in all that it *teaches*, but not everything in the Bible is meant to be understood as 'teaching.' Evangelicals prefer the word *infallible,* the belief that the Bible is fully reliable and trustworthy, especially concerning the self-revelation of God in Jesus Christ.

Authority. Because the Bible is the inspired witness to God's special revelations, it is authoritative in matters of *orthodoxy* (Christian beliefs) and *orthopraxis* (Christian practice). Many outside the Christian faith do not accept the authority of the Bible, because their worldviews do not allow for the possibility of *supernatural* revelation. Those within the faith have a different problem: not the authority of the Bible per se, but interpreting and applying its teachings to church governance, the sacraments, liturgy, missions, social justice and other matters.

Dwight: As mentioned earlier, Catholics and Protestants sometimes argue about which came first, the Bible or the church. The answer is neither. God came first, and he inspired those whom he called to record his special revelations. Where Catholics differ with Protestants is in our belief that the Catholic Church is the authoritative interpreter of the Bible, which eliminates individualistic interpretations of scripture.

> A major difference between Catholics and Protestants has to do with *authority*. In Protestantism, authority in matters of faith and practice is based on the written scriptures. Catholicism has a complementary source of authority—church-based teachings—that are deemed equally authoritative with scripture. Protestants accept many church-based teachings, but do not accord them the same weight as scripture. We will look at the basis of authority in Chapter 4.
>
> Another difference between Catholics and Protestants is that their Old Testaments have different numbers of books. The Catholic Old Testament has forty-six books; the Protestant Old Testament has thirty-nine books. The Protestant Old Testament includes only those books that were received into the Hebrew canon; the Catholic Old Testament includes, in addition to these books, several books from the *Septuagint*, the Greek translation of the Old Testament. A discussion of the Catholic and Protestant Old Testament canons is set out under canonicity in Chapter 7.

GOD THE FATHER
The Knowledge, Trinity and Attributes of God

The Knowledge of God. The knowledge of God comes to us in four ways. First, God is made known in *creation* (Romans 1:20). Reasoning from what we observe of the world around us, we arrive at a creator or author of the universe. Something cannot come from nothing; there had to have been a prime mover or first cause. Second, God is made known in *providence*—his 'provide-ence' for his people—as when he heard the cries of the Israelites in Egypt and came to their rescue. Third, God is made known in *human conscience*, which distinguishes humans from all other creatures. Human conscience enables us to discern what is right and what is wrong, and urges us to do the right and not the wrong. Fourth, and most importantly, God is made known in *Jesus*, "the image of the invisible God" (Colossians 1:15); the Word that became flesh "and lived among us" (John 1:14); "the exact representation of [God's] being" (Hebrews 1:3); the one in whom, the Danish philosopher Søren Kierkegaard said, "the infinite became finite."

The Trinity of God. Protestants and Catholics alike believe in the Trinity or *three-ness* of God—one divine corporate being in three consubstantial *personas*: the wholly other, eternal creator of the universe and of life on planet earth; his incarnate son, Jesus Christ, who came to reconcile us with his creator-father and with one another; and the indwelling Holy Spirit, who regenerates and sanctifies us. Some say that the Trinity is like sound: God is the source or *speaker*, who spoke creation into existence by his word (Isaiah 55:11); Jesus is the word *spoken* (Hebrews 1:2); and the Holy Spirit is the way God continues to *speak* (John 16:13). Others say the Trinity is like the sun, which comes to us in three different *modes*: as heat, light and energy. Still others say the Trinity is like a *rainbow*: each of the colors in a rainbow is separate and distinct from the others, but all are part of the same 'bow.'

The Attributes of God. How are we to visualize God, who is pure spirit (John 4:24)? One way to do so is to talk about God's *attributes*, those qualities that are intrinsic to God by virtue of his being God. Protestants and Catholics both agree that God is the *creator*: God created the heavens and the earth and life on earth; he created out of nothing rather than molding or forming what already was; before God there was nothing except God. Both believe that God is *eternal*: time began with God and will end with God; there was no time when God 'was not'; he is from "everlasting to everlasting" (Psalm 90:2). Both regard God as *omnipotent*: he is sovereign, supreme and all-powerful; he is able to do whatever he wishes and wills to do (Psalm 135:6); all things are under his divine rule. Both think of God as *omnipresent*: he is not limited by spatial boundaries;

he is everywhere present at one and the same time (Psalm 139:7-12). Both believe that God is *omniscient*: he is all-seeing and all-knowing (Hebrews 4:13); he is one from whom no one can hide; he knows those who love him and those who do not. Both understand God as *transcendent* and *immanent*: he is beyond and external to all that is, as in the creation of the universe; and he is present, active and close by, as in the Exodus and at Mount Sinai and in Jesus of Nazareth; he is the One in whom "we live and move and have our being" (Acts 17:28). Finally, Protestants and Catholics agree that God is a *person* who loves us and with whom we can have, through his Son, a personal relationship.

HUMANKIND
Children of God and Heirs of Adam and Eve

Man and woman are God's special creation—the crown of his creation—but Adam and Eve, the representative 'parents' or progenitors of the human race, fell into sin. And because the human race is interconnected—Augustine said we are all part of the same 'lump'—we, as their heirs, are fallen as well. God's redemption of the human race began with the call of Abraham (Genesis 12:1-3); it reached its climax with the coming of Jesus of Nazareth, who died that we "may not perish [in our sins] ... but have eternal life" (John 3:16).

The Doctrine of Sin. Sin is both a state and an action. Catholic philosopher and theologian Peter Kreeft says that sin is to the soul what disease is to the body. Our indwelt sinfulness—our sinful disease—gives rise to the commission of sinful acts, sometimes called 'actual' sins or 'daily' sins. One Greek word for sin is *hamartia*, which means 'missing the mark.' What is the mark? It is perfect *love*. We sin when we do not love God with all our heart, soul, mind and strength (Mark 12:30); when we disobey his will and commands (1 John 5:3); when we do not show love, kindness and compassion to others.

Dwight: We agree in essence that humanity is soiled by sin, but there is some disagreement between Protestants and Catholics concerning the extent of the fallen condition. Catholics believe that human beings are fundamentally good, because we are made and remain in the image of God, though this image was stained or soiled in the 'fall' in the Garden. I think Catholics and Protestants would both agree that sin brings spiritual death and can only be cleansed or healed by Christ's redeeming death on the cross. Although we agree on this, I somehow feel that Protestants are more pessimistic about sin than Catholics.

John: Reflecting on your comment about Protestants being more pessimistic about sin, I seem to recall that Catholics sing *Amazing Grace* differently than Protestants. Protestants say, "Amazing grace, how sweet the sound, that saved a wretch like me." Catholics say, "Amazing grace, how sweet the sound, that saved and strengthened me."

The world does not like the word 'sin' and rarely uses it, as psychiatrist Karl Menninger observed in his book *What Ever Happened to Sin?* Looking at the world around us, however—with its crime and violence, drug and other addictions, terrorism and war, greed and corruption in business and government, spousal abuse and child molestation, suicide bombings in the Middle East and school and drive-by shootings in the United States—it is hard to deny the all-pervasiveness of sin and evil, which have been with us since the beginning of time. The English Catholic writer G. K. Chesterton, in his autobiography *Orthodoxy*, said that sin is one Christian doctrine that no one can dispute. Chesterton said all you have to do is read the daily newspaper; today we would say that all you have to do is watch the evening news on television.

> One difference between Catholics and Protestants is the Catholic division of sins into 'venial,' from the Latin *venia*, meaning forgivable or pardonable, and 'mortal' or deadly, which, unless forgiven and absolved by a priest, can result in one losing his or her salvation. We will look at the forgiveness of sins in our discussion of the sacrament of reconciliation in Chapter 6.
>
> Another difference between Catholics and most Protestants is the Catholic belief that original sin is washed away or removed when one is baptized ("Repent, and be baptized ... so that your sins may be forgiven," Acts 2:38). Some Protestants also believe this, but most understand baptism as a sign or symbol of one's new life in Christ.

JESUS CHRIST
The Incarnate Son of God

Jesus' Virginal Conception. The virginal conception of Jesus in Mary's womb is set forth in the Matthean and Lukan birth narratives. They do not *prove* Jesus' miraculous conception; rather, they *announce* that Jesus was God-incarnate (God-in-the-flesh) from the very beginning. How did this occur? Or to ask Mary's question, "How can this be, since I am a virgin?" (Luke 1:34). Matthew and Luke tell us in their birth narratives that it occurred through the agency or power of the Holy Spirit. Luke, who said that he "investigated everything carefully" (Luke 1:3), may have learned about Jesus' conception and birth from Mary during his stay in Caesarea when Paul was imprisoned there in the late 50s (Mary is believed to have lived into the 60s).

There has been an ongoing effort over the past two centuries to demythologize miracles such as the virgin birth, which is a stumbling block for non-Christians, and even for some Christians. British scholar Keith Ward said the strongest argument for the veracity of the Matthean and Lukan birth narratives is that it is impossible to believe they would have been invented when their claim—that a child conceived out of wedlock was the genetic, anointed, messianic descendant of King David—would have been so offensive to Jewish ears.

> A major difference between Catholics and Protestants regarding Jesus' virgin birth is that, while Protestants affirm the virginal conception of Jesus, most deny Catholic teaching that Mary was a *perpetual* virgin, meaning that she was a virgin before, during and after Jesus' birth. We will look at this when we look at Catholicism's Marian doctrines in Chapter 5.

Jesus: Fully Divine, Fully Human. Catholics and Protestants believe that Jesus was both fully divine ("conceived by the Holy Spirit") and fully human ("born of the Virgin Mary"). Jesus' humanity can be seen in the accounts of his life: he was born of a woman; ate with friends and sinners and went to weddings; preached to crowds and debated the Pharisees; was often weary and sorrowful and at times even angry; and he suffered, died and was buried. As for Jesus' divinity, he was conceived by the Holy Spirit, thus by God himself; performed miracles, which pointed to his divinity; had divine foreknowledge, as shown in his knowledge of Nathaniel (John 1:47-52) and reading the minds of the scribes when he healed the paralytic (Mark 2:6-12); claimed 'oneness' with God (John 10:30 and John 14:11), meaning that he and God were one in essence or nature, not two identical persons; and he claimed prerogatives of God, such as forgiving sin (Mark 2:5).

Salvation
By Grace, Through Faith

The fundamental question of every religious person is the question of the Philippian jailer in the book of Acts: "What must I do to be saved?" (Acts 16:30). Both Catholics and Protestants would agree with Paul's answer: "Believe on the Lord Jesus" (Acts 16:31).

Grace and Faith. Protestants and Catholics alike believe that we are saved "by grace ... through faith" (Ephesians 2:8). The first part of the equation is God's gift of *grace*, Jesus' death 'for us,' which is free. There is nothing that we can do to earn our salvation, nothing that will oblige God to save us. But for God's gift of salvation to be effective, it must be accepted. This is the second part of the equation. We are saved *through faith* in Jesus Christ. This means believing, trusting and confessing Jesus as our Savior and living under his lordship.

> Though both Catholics and Protestants believe that we are saved by grace through faith, there is a difference between the two having to do with the exclusivity of faith. Protestants believe that we are saved by faith *alone*. Catholics believe that faith, to be *saving* faith, must be accompanied by observing the sacraments, through which God's grace flows, and doing works of love and charity. We will look at the means and assurance of salvation in Chapter 4.

Jesus' Saving Death. Karl Barth, the most influential Protestant theologian of the twentieth century, said the most important word in the New Testament is the Greek word *huper*, which means 'on behalf of.' Jesus died for us—for our inability to save ourselves. In ancient Israel, priests sacrificed animals time and again to cover the sins of the people (Leviticus 1-7). The prophet Isaiah said one is coming who will bear the sins of the people in his own *body* (Isaiah 53). Jesus told his disciples at the Last Supper that Isaiah's prophecy "must be fulfilled in me" (Luke 22:37), for he came "not to be served but to serve and to give his life as a ransom for many" (Mark 10:45).

THE HOLY SPIRIT
Gifts, Regeneration and Sanctification

Catholics and Protestants both believe in the Holy Spirit, or Holy Ghost, from the Old English word *gast*, meaning 'spirit.' The Holy Spirit is the third person of the Trinity, thus a *person*, not some vague, impersonal force. Jesus was conceived through the power of the Holy Spirit (Luke 1:35); he was anointed by the Spirit at his baptism (Luke 3:21-22); he prayed to his Father in the name of the Spirit; and he promised his followers that God would send the Spirit upon them after his departure (John 16:7).

Gifts. One function of the Holy Spirit is to grant specific *gifts* to believers, some twenty of which are mentioned in Paul's letters in the New Testament. Among them are the gifts of faith, knowledge, healing, miracles, prophecy, discernment, speaking in 'tongues' (called *glossalalia*, usually a language not known to the speaker), exhortation, teaching and generosity. Paul's lists of gifts are not meant to be all-inclusive, because each time he mentions gifts he adds to the list of gifts in his previous letters. According to the New Testament, every believer has at least *one gift* of the Spirit (1 Corinthians 12:7 and 1 Peter 4:10).

Regeneration and Sanctification. Repentance is the first step in coming to faith, though Christians disagree about *how* we come to faith. Some say that belief is a conscious human choice and act. Jesus says, in the book of Revelation, "I stand at the door and knock [waiting to be invited in]" (Revelation 3:20). Others say the ability "to repent and believe the good news" (Mark 1:15) comes from a God-given prevenient ('coming before') gift of grace. The steps beyond repentance are regeneration and sanctification. *Regeneration* is something that God does through the power of the Holy Spirit, the power that enables us to be 'born again' or 'born from above' (John 3:1-10). Being regenerated, however, does not mean that we no longer sin; concupiscence, the inborn tendency to sin, continues to persist. Rather, it means that we are no longer controlled by sin or slaves to sin. *Sanctification* is the continuing work of the Holy Spirit that enables believers to grow in obedience to God and in righteousness.

How do we receive the Holy Spirit? Catholics and sacramental Protestants believe that we receive the Holy Spirit at baptism. Non-sacramental Baptists, Brethren, Pentecostals and others believe that the Spirit is received when one publicly professes one's faith in Jesus as Lord and Savior.

> One difference between Catholics and Protestants is that most sacramental Protestants believe that one receives the Spirit in all his fullness when one is baptized. Catholics seem to believe in a two-step process: one receives the Spirit at baptism, which is 'sealed' when one is confirmed. We will look at this in our discussion of baptism and confirmation in Chapter 6.

THE CHURCH
One, Holy, Universal and Apostolic

The Nicene Creed sets forth four *marks* of the church, which both Catholics and Protestants agree upon. First, the church is *one*—"one body … one Spirit … one Lord … one God and Father of all" (Ephesians 4:4-6). Being one, however, does not mean that the church must everywhere be uniform, a qualification that allows for differences in church governance and forms of worship. Second, the church is *holy*, which does not mean pious or sacred, but separate, distinct and set apart for ministry in and to the world. Third, the church is catholic, a Greek word meaning *universal* and worldwide. Fourth, the church is *apostolic*, meaning the church founded by Jesus' apostles and his commissioning of them to make him known "to the ends of the earth" (Acts 1:8).

Dwight: While Catholics and Protestants agree that the church is *one*, Catholics mean more than Protestants mean. Catholics believe that there is an external unity among *all* Catholics, and that there is a mystical one-ness in Catholicism that is both 'visible'—the community of believers on earth, and 'invisible'— the community of the 'saved,' who are known only by God.

Also, when Catholics say that the church is *apostolic*, we mean more than Protestants do. We believe that the bishops of the Catholic Church are the 'successors' of the apostles, a succession that comes through an unbroken chain of the laying on of hands in the consecration of bishops. Because bishops are the successors of the apostles, they speak with the same authority as did the apostles, except for those privileges that were given to and enjoyed only by the apostles themselves. I know this is a major claim, but this is what Catholics mean by this phrase in the creed.

An ecclesiastical difference between Catholicism and Protestantism has to do with church polity or governance. Catholic polity is 'episcopal' or hierarchical, with the pope having authority over the worldwide church, bishops having authority over ecclesiastical dioceses, and priests in charge of local parishes. Some Protestant denominations have an episcopal or hierarchical polity—Anglicans and Lutherans, for instance—but none has a supreme pontiff. Two popular forms of Protestant polity are *presbyterian*, found in Reformed and Presbyterian churches, with the leadership residing in

> 'presbyteries' composed of clergypersons and elders within a district or region; and congregational or *free*, found in Baptist, Brethren, Covenant, Assemblies of God, Evangelical Free and Congregational churches, with authority residing in the laity rather than in bishops or presbyteries.

THE END TIMES
Resurrection, Intermediate State and Eternity

Protestants and Catholics alike have a linear, hope-filled view of history, as opposed to the ancient Greek view that history is cyclical, like the seasons of the year; or the Hindu and Buddhist view that history is illusory; or the secular view that history is a series of unconnected events without meaning, 'just one thing after another going nowhere.' Christians believe that there will be an *end time* when Christ will return (John 14:3), the dead will be raised (John 5:28-29) and all will be judged (2 Corinthians 5:10). As we learn in John 3:16—sometimes called 'the Gospel within the Gospels'—there will be two outcomes: those who believe in Jesus will receive *everlasting life* and live in God's final, perfected kingdom; those who do not believe will *perish* and be separated from God forever.

The period between death and resurrection is called the Intermediate State, about which the New Testament tells us, one Protestant writer said, "little more than a whisper." Some Christians believe that both body and soul perish until Jesus returns. Others believe that we go immediately to heaven, based on Jesus' statement to the so-called good thief on the cross: "Today you will be with me in paradise" (Luke 23:43). Still others believe that the soul separates from the body and lives on until the body is resurrected. Theologians who hold this view assume that the soul goes to a place that is permanent and eternal, but remains incomplete until Jesus returns and gathers up all who have believed. Then, so the argument continues, the soul takes up residence in a new, resurrected body.

> One difference between Catholics and Protestants has to do with purgatory, the Catholic belief that those who die with unforgiven *venial* sins must have their sins purged before proceeding on to heaven. Protestants believed that we are saved by Jesus' death on the cross, which does not require any post-death cleansing. We will look at this in our discussion of purgatory in Chapter 7.

The twin pillars underlying Protestantism are *sola scriptura* and *sola fide*. In the next chapter we will look at *sola scriptura* and the Catholic belief in tradition, which Catholics view as being equally authoritative with scripture. We will also look at the Protestant belief in salvation by faith *alone*, and the Catholic belief that observing the sacraments and doing works of love and charity are necessary for one's faith to be salvific, that is, sufficient for salvation.

CHAPTER FOUR

Never the Twain Shall Meet

Sola Scriptura and Sola Fide

There is a double 'continental divide' between Catholics and Protestants. The first has to do with the source of authority in matters of faith and practice. For Protestants, the source of authority is the Bible and the Bible *alone*. For Catholics, there is a second source of authority, namely, church-based tradition. Some say there is even a third authority, the Magisterium, which interprets both scripture and tradition. The second 'divide' has to do with the means and assurance of salvation. In Protestantism, salvation comes through God's grace, which is received by *faith* (Ephesians 2:8). In Catholicism, grace comes through the sacraments; and faith, to be salvific, must express itself in acts of love and charity.

THE BASIS OF AUTHORITY
The Word of God
The word of God first came as spoken words to prophets and apostles called by God to speak his words to humankind. It was only later—in the case of the Hebrew scriptures, hundreds of years later—that these 'words' were written down and gathered together to form our Old and New Testaments. Catholics believe that God *also* spoke in ways that were not written in scripture. In the Fourth Gospel, the author writes, "This is the disciple [John] who is testifying to these

things and has written them down ... There are also many *other things* that Jesus did [and said]; if every one of them were written down ... the world itself could not contain the books that would be written" (John 21:25). In Catholicism, these 'other things' constitute tradition.

Tradition is one of the least developed and most controversial aspects of Catholic theology. Catholic scholars talk about the 'college of the apostles' and the 'college of bishops.' The term *college*, in this context, means a body of persons having a common interest and duty, like the Electoral College, which elects the president of the United States, and the College of Cardinals, which elects the pope. In Catholic theology, the college of apostles received the word of God. A large portion of what was revealed was written down to form what later came to be the New Testament. The rest was passed on, through the agency of the Holy Spirit, to the college of bishops to make God's revelations clear and understandable. Thus, in Catholicism, there are two sources of authority: written scripture and unwritten tradition. Both are seen as revelations of God and equally authoritative in matters of faith and practice.

One of the confusing things about tradition is that there are two kinds of 'tradition.' The first is capital 'T' tradition. Capital T tradition refers to the content of that which has been handed on from the apostles to the bishops and underlies Catholic *dogmas* (official, authoritative teachings). The second kind is small 't' tradition-based teachings, which are neither dogma nor doctrinal. Examples are church liturgy, feast days, the use of the rosary, sacramentals such as holy water and incense, and the celibacy of priests. This chapter is concerned only with capital T tradition.

Dwight: You make it sound like tradition is unique to Catholicism. Every religion has some form of tradition, even Protestantism. Baptist, Lutheran, Presbyterian, Methodist and other denominations place a great deal of weight on the teachings and biblical interpretations they inherited from their ancestors in the faith.

Protestants revere, preserve and rely on handed-down tradition just as much as Catholics do.

John: Protestants follow the teachings of the founders and theologians of their denominations, Dwight, but they are not considered as having the same authority as scripture. In Protestantism, there is only *one* source of authority, the Bible, not two.

Protestantism: *Sola Scriptura*. In Protestantism, as has been mentioned several times, authority is based on the written word of God, which goes back to Martin Luther. In 1519, at Leipzig, Germany, Luther debated Johannes Eck, one of the Catholic Church's leading theologians and most skillful orators. Their debate was about *authority*. Westminster Seminary professor of church history Robert Godfrey, in his book *Reformation Sketches*, said that "Eck kept pressing the point that Luther could not be right when he stood against the popes, the doctors, the bishops, the councils and the tradition of the church. What right did he have to claim that he was right and everyone else was wrong?" Eck painted Luther into a corner. Luther was a professor of biblical studies and turned to the only thing he knew—the Bible—to defend his writings, out of which evolved the Protestant doctrine of *sola scriptura*.

Protestantism accepts tradition-based teachings that are based on scripture. Luke tells us that his 'orderly account' came from reports that were "*handed on to us* by those who from the beginning were eyewitnesses and servants of the word" (Luke 1:2). Material that is 'handed on' refers to tradition. Paul tells the Thessalonians to "Stand firm and hold on to the *traditions* that were taught to us, either by word of mouth or by our letter" (2 Thessalonians 2:15). Paul here affirms the validity of tradition. In a very famous passage in Paul's first letter to the church at Corinth, Paul says, "I *handed on* to you as of first importance what I had *received*" (1 Corinthians 15:3). Paul affirms the validity of traditions he received from others, which he passed on to the church in Corinth as a matter of "first importance." When handed-on tradition was written down and accepted as canonical scripture, it became authoritative in matters of belief and practice.

Protestantism also accepts doctrines that came long after tradition-based teachings were written down and received into the canon. Protestants accept the declaration of the Council of Nicea in 325, which stated that Jesus was the "very God of very God"; they accept the decision of the Council of Chalcedon in 451, which declared that Jesus was both fully human and fully divine; and they accept the doctrine of the Trinity, which was expounded by Tertullian in the third century and put in final form by Augustine in the fourth century.

Protestants accept the decisions of Nicea and Chalcedon and doctrines like the Trinity because they have underlying scriptural support. The Nicene Creed's statement that Jesus *was* God—that is, part of the triune Godhead—rather than merely *similar* to God, is set out in the prologue to John's Gospel: "In the beginning was the Word ... and the Word was God ... and the Word became flesh" (1:1; 1:14). The Chalcedon Council declared that Christ was both fully human and fully divine comes from Luke's birth narrative: "The angel said to [Mary], 'the Holy Spirit will come upon you ... and you will be with child and give birth to a son'" (1:30; 1:35). The triune nature of God is set out in several places in the New Testament; for instance, in Jesus' statement to his disciples to "Go ... and make disciples of all nations, baptizing them in the name of the Father, and of the Son and of the Holy Spirit" (Matthew 28:19).

Protestants object to doctrines that have no underlying scriptural support to authenticate their validity. Many are simply claims of the Catholic Church, which is circular reasoning: the Church claiming validity for its own teachings. Furthermore, many Catholic tradition-based beliefs seem at odds with scripture: for instance, the claim that the pope is infallible when speaking *ex cathedra*; that Mary was born without sin and upon her death was bodily assumed into heaven; and that receiving the sacraments is necessary for salvation.

Dwight: When you say that the Catholic Church's reasoning is circular, because all we have to go on is "the Catholic Church claiming validity for its own teachings," you assume that this is all the evidence we have to offer. I will show, as we go along, that there are good scriptural and theological reasons for believing Catholic tradition-based beliefs to be true.

John: How did the Catholic Church's beliefs in Mary's immaculate conception and her assumption into heaven arise, given that neither is taught in the New Testament? Did the advocates of these beliefs receive some later, post-apostolic, special revelation?

Dwight: Before I can answer your question, I have to explain the different way that Catholics and Protestants understand scriptural authority. I know this is a generalization, but Protestants often view scripture as a sourcebook for their beliefs. The assumption is that if the Bible clearly teaches something, then it must be so; and if it doesn't, then it must not be so. This method of interpretation doesn't really work, even for Protestants, because the Bible is silent about many things. As a result, Protestants have to draw their own conclusions, and they often disagree with one another about, for instance, how one gets saved, and whether or not one can lose his or her salvation, and what happens at death. Although Protestants believe in the simplicity and clarity of scripture, in fact they are forced to rely on subtle interpretations and handed-down tradition in order to answer theology's great riddles.

Catholics do the same. The church pondered the mysteries of the Incarnation, the person and role of Mary, and other matters. As it did so, it turned time and again not only to the scriptures, but also to the wisdom and learning of church fathers and others who had gone before. Catholic tradition-based dogmas and doctrines do not contradict scripture; rather, much like the doctrine of the Trinity, which is not explicitly set forth in the New Testament, they are inferred from scripture.

Catholic beliefs about Mary are based on the church's belief about her son, Jesus. In reflecting on the Incarnation, Christian theologians as early as the second century began referring to Mary as 'the second Eve' and 'all Holy.' It is from this early Christian belief that the Catholic Church came to believe that Mary was conceived by a special act of God, without the stain of original sin. Believing this to be so, they also concluded that Mary must not have suffered the corruption of death and was taken bodily to heaven, like Elijah.

John: But is it not correct to say that Catholicism has two *sources* of authority? The *Dei Verbum* document that came out of Vatican II, which we will look at when we come to the Magisterium, talks about both scripture and tradition.

Dwight: You might say there are two sources of authority, a primary source, the scriptures, and a secondary source, tradition, which brings forth the full meaning of scripture. In this regard, Catholicism is much like Judaism, which also has two bases of authority. The Jews have their scriptures, the Hebrew canon, and they also have the Talmud, the written interpretation of the scriptures. Another example might be the United States Constitution and the Supreme Court—the written Constitution and the opinions of the court in interpreting the Constitution. The Catholic Church's teaching office, the Magisterium, interprets the Bible much like the Supreme Court interprets the Constitution.

John: Being a lawyer, I like your Constitution-Supreme Court analogy, though I don't regard the post-apostolic writings of the fathers and doctors of the church and its various councils as carrying the same weight as those that came from the hands of the apostles.

Is there an easy, assessable summary of Catholic tradition-based beliefs that one can appeal to, for instance, as one can the Bible?

Dwight: The best summary would be the *Catechism of the Catholic Church*, which was released in 1994. There you will find Catholic dogmas, doctrines and teachings, with biblical texts and references to church documents down through the ages, as well as the writings of theologians and the saints. If something is in the *Catechism*, it is official Catholic doctrine; if it is not in the *Catechism*, it is not Catholic teaching.

Catholicism: Scripture and Tradition. Catholics believe that the scriptures are God's word to his people, but they are not God's *only* word to his people. God's 'other' words were passed on by the Holy Spirit from the apostles to the bishops and are, thus, equally authoritative with scripture. The Protestant claim that the Bible is the sole source of authority comes from the apostle Paul, who said that "All scripture is inspired by God" (2 Timothy 3:16). The word *inspired* means 'God-breathed.' Protestants say that only the scriptures are God-breathed; nowhere is it said that tradition is God-breathed. Catholics answer that 2 Timothy 3:16 merely says "all scripture" is inspired; it does not say that tradition-based teachings are *not* inspired or God-breathed.

The following are the names of bishops, scholars, popes and councils whose writings and pronouncements later came to be codified as Catholic dogmas and doctrines.

- *Clement of Rome* (c. 100), the third bishop of Rome, held that the Roman church had authority over all other churches.

- *Irenaeus* (c. 130-200), the bishop of Lyons, following Clement, affirmed the primacy of Rome.

- *Jerome* (342-420), the great linguist and translator of the Hebrew and Greek scriptures into Latin (the *Vulgate*), wrote in support of the belief that Mary was a perpetual virgin.

- *Ambrose* (339-397), the bishop of Milan and the mentor of Augustine, claimed that Christian marriage is indissoluble.

- *Augustine* (354-430), the bishop of Hippo (North Africa), the most important theologian in the first thousand years of Christianity, shaped the church's thinking regarding the Trinity and the church as the channel of God's grace, and he taught that marriage is a sacrament.

- Popes *Leo I* (400-461) and *Gregory I* (540-604) consolidated the primacy of the bishop of Rome over the church.

- *John of Damascus* (c. 675-749), the last of the great Eastern fathers, was the first to formally teach that Mary was assumed bodily into heaven.

- *Peter Lombard* (1095-1169), who was born in Lombardy and became the bishop of Paris, stated that the sacraments were not only signs or symbols of grace, but the 'very cause of grace,' and he regarded extreme unction (now called anointing the sick) as a sacrament.

- *William of Ockham* [England] (1285-1349), a medieval Franciscan scholar and theologian, formally advocated a double or two-source theory of revelation, scripture and tradition.

- *Thomas Aquinas* (1225-1274), the greatest philosopher and theologian of the Middle Ages, developed confirmation into a sacrament.

- *John Duns Scotus* (1266-1308), the Scottish (the word *Scotus* means 'the Scot') Franciscan, championed the church's belief in Mary's immaculate conception.

- *The Council of Trent* (1545-1563), responding to the Protestant Reformers, confirmed that there were seven sacraments, not two; affirmed the divine inspiration of the *Septuagint* and included twelve of its books in its Old Testament canon; made transubstantiation and purgatory official church dogma; and strengthened the power and office of the pope.

- *Pope Pius IX* in 1854 defined as Catholic dogma that Mary was conceived 'immaculate,' that is, without sin.

- *Vatican I* (1870) affirmed that the pope, when speaking *ex cathedra* on matters of faith and morals, speaks without error.

- *Pope Pius XII*, speaking *ex cathedra* in 1950, declared as an article of faith for all Catholics that Mary was assumed 'body and soul' into heaven.

- *Vatican II* (1962-65), following Trent, declared that "both scripture and tradition should be accepted with equal sentiments of devotion and reverence."

The above 'sources' of Catholic tradition includes five popes (Clement of Rome, Leo the Great, Gregory the Great, Pius IX and Pius XII), four bishops (Irenaeus, Ambrose, Augustine and Peter Lombard), five scholars (Jerome, John of Damascus, William of Ockham, Thomas Aquinas and John Duns Scotus) and three councils (Trent, Vatican I and Vatican II).

John: Many of the teachings above seem like 'human' teachings—those of Jerome, Ambrose, Augustine, John of Damascus, Aquinas and others—not divine revelation. Furthermore, according to Cardinal John Henry Newman, "No one can add to revelation. That was given once and for all." How does Newman's comment square with the Catholic Church's claim that post-apostolic tradition-based teachings are revelatory in nature and authoritative as scripture?

Dwight: Newman is right: we cannot add to God's revelation. This ended with the death of the last apostle. Catholics believe that we better understand God's revelation as time goes on. As new challenges unfold, the Holy Spirit guides us "into all truth," as Jesus promised in John 16:13. The writings of scholars and theologians and the declarations of church bodies and councils come from the prompting of the Holy Spirit and are authenticated by the Magisterium, which we will look at shortly.

When a doctrinal dispute arises, it is the bishops in council with the pope who, by the power of the Holy Spirit, define church teachings so they can be understood by the people. The bishops and the pope do this through a long process of consultation and discussion. When Popes Pius IX and Pius XII pronounced the two most modern dogmas—Mary's immaculate conception and her assumption into heaven—they did so after consultation with Catholic bishops around the world. Contrary to popular belief, these dogmas were not papal decrees from on high; they evolved upward from a groundswell of Catholic opinion, which the Magisterium carefully considered and approved.

The Magisterium. A third 'authority' in Catholicism is the Magisterium, from the Latin *magister*, meaning 'master,' as in master teacher. The Magisterium is the teaching office of the Catholic Church; it is comprised of Catholic bishops and the pope. The Magisterium interprets and pronounces what scripture and tradition mean. According to *Dei Verbum* (*The Word of God*), the Dogmatic Constitution on the Divine Revelation promulgated by Pope Paul VI in 1965, "The task of interpreting the Word of God has been entrusted exclusively to the Church," that is, to the Magisterium. Furthermore, Vatican II said, "Sacred Tradition, Holy Scripture and the Church's Magisterium are by God's most wise decree so closely connected and associated together that one does not subsist without the other two." The role of the Magisterium is to interpret and articulate the teachings of both scripture and tradition.

Dwight: Scripture is not always and everywhere clear, as in the story of Philip and the Ethiopian, who was reading Isaiah 53 and said, "How can I [understand what I am reading] unless someone explains it to me?" (Acts 8:26-34). If the Bible is easy to understand, as some Protestants claim, why are there so many different Protestant versions of the Bible? And why do scholars often disagree with one another as to the meaning of scripture? And why do different denominations appeal to the same scriptures to support their beliefs?

Catholicism has a central, unified, interpretative authority, the Magisterium. We believe that having a central authority is preferable to leaving matters in the hands of denominational bodies and individual churches. If there is no central, official authority, everything is up for grabs. In Protestantism, some believe that the Bible is inerrant, but most do not; some say the sacraments convey grace, others say they are only symbols of grace; some baptize infants, others only adults; some say that Christ is mystically present in the bread and wine, others that the Lord's Supper is only a memorial.

John: Having a central authority is good in theory, but the teachings of the Catholic Church are not universally followed. Former Catholic-turned-evangelical James McCarthy, in his book *The Gospel According to Rome*, says, "The beliefs of some [Catholics] are so diverse that the term 'Cafeteria Catholics' has been coined to describe the way they pick and choose what they believe." (The same is also true, unfortunately, of many Protestants.) Although anyone can read the Bible, am I correct in saying that only the Magisterium has the right to interpret the scriptures?

Dwight: The Magisterium is a God-given vehicle for the service of the people of God. Its role is to address difficulties, resolve disputes and correct errors. Anyone can interpret the scriptures in the Catholic Church, but the last and final word rests with the Magisterium to assure that interpretations of scripture are faithful to the word of God and without error.

John: I understand that the Holy Spirit protects the Magisterium from committing error. How does this work?

Dwight: The Holy Spirit guides the bishops while they are deliberating to keep their pronouncements free from error, and here we are talking only about statements relating to matters of faith and morals and, happily, this is not defined too closely. Catholics are expected to listen to the Church's teachings and to respond with open minds and hearts in a spirit of loving obedience.

Many Catholics, especially American Catholics, wish that the Catholic Church would soften its positions on abortion, sexual issues, the marriage of priests, the ordination of women and other matters. The Catholic Church teaches what is true to scripture, not what is popular. Protestant churches that have softened their stands on historic beliefs are dying; those that are growing and vibrant are those that have remained faithful to their scripture-based traditions and teachings.

John: I have heard that the Magisterium is made up of the bishops of the Catholic Church, but that, actually, the decisions of the Magisterium come from a very small body of men around the pope. Is this true, or do all bishops—some 5,000 today—participate in and have an active voice in the decisions of the Magisterium?

Dwight: Bishops worldwide, in council with the pope, make up the Magisterium, though I doubt whether all 5,000 bishops participate in the decision-making process. Sometimes the decision-making goes even beyond the bishops. For instance, on something revolutionary, like cloning or *in vitro* fertilization, the Magisterium consults with world experts, academics and theologians to guide the church in making decisions that are faithful to scripture.

THE MEANS AND ASSURANCE OF SALVATION

Many think that the central teaching of the Reformation was *sola scriptura*. Actually, the central teaching was justification or salvation by grace alone through faith alone. The basis for this teaching was

Martin Luther's understanding of God's righteousness in Paul's letter to the church at Rome: "[The gospel] is the power of God for salvation to everyone who has faith … For in it the righteousness of God is revealed through faith for faith" (Romans 1:16-17).

Protestantism: *Sole Fide*. According to some in the Middle Ages, God's righteousness had to be *satisfied* for one to be saved. How was this possible? By doing faithful works of prayer, fasting, service to others, confession and observing the sacraments. Try as he could, Luther never felt himself worthy before God. While studying Paul's letter to the Romans, Luther came to understand that 'righteousness' is not something that God *demands* from us; rather, it is something that he *gives* to us in Christ. Thus we are not saved by what we can do for God, but what God has done for us in Christ.

When Luther came to his breakthrough understanding of how we are put right with God, he said, "I felt that I was altogether born again and had entered paradise itself through open gates." Luther's epiphany is referred to as his Tower Experience, because it came to him in the Wittenberg Tower. Luther had committed much of the Bible to memory, including the whole of the New Testament. As he thought through the scriptures, he slowly came to realize that salvation was by *grace alone,* God's free gift of grace in Jesus Christ; through *faith alone,* the means by which we appropriate God's grace and are justified or saved.

Catholicism: Faith, Sacraments and Works. Catholicism maintains that salvation is by grace alone, but not through *faith* alone. It holds that faith must be accompanied by observing the sacraments and doing works of love and charity, as set forth in the *Catechism of the Catholic Church.*

- "Faith is *necessary* for salvation" (Article 183).
- "The Church affirms that for believers the sacraments of the New Covenant are *necessary* for salvation" (Article 1129).

- "Service of and witness to the faith are *necessary* for salvation" (Article 1816).

John: John 3:16 says that whoever *believes* in Jesus shall not perish but have eternal life. It does not say "whoever believes ... and *observes the sacraments* and *does works of service* will have eternal life." In Protestantism, believing in Jesus' atoning, sacrificial death is sufficient for salvation. Adding the sacraments and works suggests that, for Catholics, faith is not enough. Am I correct about this?

Dwight: This is an argument from silence, John. We're not debating the fact that whoever believes in Jesus will have eternal life. We both believe that. In your case, though, you seem to be missing what the rest of John's Gospel and the other books in the New Testament clearly teach: that faithful obedience to Jesus' teachings and God's commandments are evidence of the fullness and firmness of one's faith. Salvation is not mental assent to doctrinal propositions; it is the total commitment and transformation of one's life, which means a life of action and good works.

John: In requiring the observance of the sacraments and doing works of service and charity, it seems like Catholics are required to participate in the process of salvation. Is this true?

Dwight: We believe that the sacraments are God's work toward us, not, as you imply, our work toward God. We believe the sacraments are necessary for salvation because this is what Jesus himself taught. Regarding the sacrament of baptism, Jesus said, "I tell you, no one can enter the kingdom of God without being born of water and Spirit" (John 3:5). The Catholic Church has always understood this to teach the necessity of baptism. Regarding the sacrament of Holy Eucharist, Jesus said, "I tell you, unless you eat the flesh of the Son of Man and drink his blood, you have no life in you" (John 6:53). This passage teaches the necessity of observing the Eucharist or Lord's Supper.

We also believe that it is necessary to witness to the faith; so did Jesus. In Matthew 28:19-20, the Great Commission, Jesus tells his disciples that they are to "Go forth and make disciples of all nations ['all people']." He also said, "Everyone who acknowledges me before others, I also will acknowledge before my Father in heaven; but whoever denies me before others, I also will deny before my Father in heaven" (Matthew 10:32-33). Catholics are called to witness to their faith.

Furthermore, we believe that it is necessary to perform good works in order to be saved. So did Jesus, as expressed in his parable of the sheep and the goats, when he said, "[Whatever] you did for one the least of these … you did for me" (Matthew 25:40). The New Testament is full of this sort of language. From Matthew to John to Paul to James, we read that the final judgment will be based on how we have performed acts of love and charity. This does not mean that we are saved *by* good works; it means that we cannot be saved *without* good works. This is solid Catholic teaching.

Protestants believe that Christ's saving death is *imputed*—attributed or credited—to the believer. When one accepts the finished work of Christ on the cross and "puts on the Lord Jesus Christ" (Romans 13:14)—that is, is made one with Christ—he or she is at that moment *declared* righteous. Catholics believe that justification is a *process*—an infusion of grace, which begins with baptism and continues as one observes the sacraments, especially the Eucharist—rather than a one-time, declarative act. In Catholicism, justification refers to the seed that God plants in a believer's heart, which grows by observing the sacraments and the indwelling Holy Spirit and changes men and women into righteous beings acceptable to God. Further, Catholics believe that for one's faith to be salvific, the believer must do works of service and charity, which differs from the Protestant view that "a person is justified by faith apart from works" (Romans 3:28). Catholics say that when Paul talks about 'works,' he means that salvation does not come through our own works or efforts. Furthermore, such 'works' are not done to secure merits for oneself, but to honor God.

Catholics say that the Protestant understanding of justification is a legal fiction: declaring one to be righteous without any ongoing work or effort on the part of the believer. This is an incorrect understanding of 'faith alone.' Protestantism believes that one is justified, that is, declared righteous, by faith; and having been justified, one is called to live out his or her faith by doing the good works James refers to in his letter (2:14-26) and Paul mentions in Ephesians 2:10. Protestants, just as much as Catholics, believe that one's faith, to be saving faith, must be real, genuine and authentic. Martin Luther said that "faith without works is a false faith and does not justify." Referring to himself, he said, "I do not do good works to be declared righteous; rather, being declared righteous I do good works." Protestants believe that salvation is more than intellectual assent to Jesus' salvific death. The German theologian and martyr Dietrich Bonhoeffer called this 'cheap grace': the belief that because Christ died for us, we don't have to do anything ourselves.

Dwight: You've expressed what I also believe. Luther's view is close to the Catholic view. Both sides agree that faith is necessary, and both sides agree that true faith must be accompanied by actions of faith. This is affirmed in Hebrews 11, the New Testament's 'Faith Hall of Fame.' This chapter hammers home, with example after example, that men of faith were men who performed faithful acts.

The Assurance of Salvation. A second difference between Catholics and Protestants regarding salvation is the assurance of salvation. Protestants take comfort in Jesus' words that "Everyone who looks to the Son and believes in him shall have eternal life, and I will raise him [her] up on the last day" (John 6:40); and Paul's words that "If you confess with your mouth, 'Jesus is Lord,' and believe in your heart that God raised him from the dead, you will be saved" (Romans 10:9).

John: In your book *Challenging Catholics*, Dwight, you said, "[Catholics] believe no one can know for sure if they are saved eternally, because God alone is our judge." Is this the Catholic position? Is there is no assurance of salvation in Catholicism?

Dwight: Catholics believe in the mercy and omnipotence of God, who transforms sinners and strengthens the justified. We do not live in anxious trepidation about damnation; we are much more concerned about loving God than avoiding hell. If we trust in Jesus Christ, and continue to live in his grace and follow his teachings, and try to avoid sins that might separate us from his love, we have every confidence that we will one day join him in heaven. The hope and confidence we have is not in our ability to love God and obey his commandments. Our hope is in God's infinite mercy and justice, and in his Son, who died to save us.

Catholicism's view that tradition is authoritative underlies many of its distinctive beliefs. In the next three chapters we will look at several of these, among them the papacy, Mary, the sacraments and purgatory. The authors hope that their dialogue will help Catholics and Protestants better understand the historical and scriptural reasons for their respective beliefs.

CHAPTER FIVE

Peter, Paul and Mary:

The Papacy and the Virgin Mary

The Catholic Church believes that its bishops are the successors of the original apostles and stand in an unbroken line of 'apostolic succession' from Peter to the present day; that the bishop of Rome, the pope, is Christ's vicar or representative on earth; and that the pope is infallible when he speaks on matters of faith and morals. The Catholic Church also believes that Mary was conceived 'immaculate,' that is, without sin; that she was a perpetual virgin, meaning before, during and after Jesus' birth; and that upon her death she was assumed body and soul into heaven. Protestants find no scriptural support for any of these six beliefs.

THE POPE
Christ's Vicar on Earth

When I grew up, Pius XII (papal reign: 1939-1958) was the pope. I used to see pictures of him in newsreels in theaters and in the newspapers in his white vestments, miter and shepherd's staff. It was front page news when a pope died and cardinals from around the world went to Rome and met in the Sistine Chapel to elect a new pope, sending black and white smoke signals to say that they had or had not selected a new pope. (Twice-a-day ballots are taken in these gatherings, called conclaves. The ballots are burned, along with straw, to send signals to those outside; adding chemicals to the straw produces black smoke.) This still goes on, as we saw with the April 2005 four-ballot election of Cardinal Ratzinger as the 265th bishop of Rome. Popes serve for life, unless they resign, which has happened on three occasions.

Catholics believe that the pope is the vicar of Christ. The word *vicar* comes from the word *vicarious*, meaning 'one who represents another.' Catholicism bases its Peter-the-vicar teaching on Jesus' words, "You are Peter, and on this rock I will build my church ... and I will give you the keys [the symbol of authority] of the kingdom of heaven" (Matthew 16:18-19). Catholics read these verses as evidence that Jesus bestowed upon Peter the leadership of the church. The words "on this rock," however, must be read in context. Jesus has just asked his disciples, "Who do you say that I am?" Peter answers, "You are the Messiah, the Son of the living God." Most Protestants understand "on this rock" to refer to Peter's *rock-like confession*. This was also the view of most Christians during the first thousand years of the church, according to Protestant scholar Keith Mathison, in his book *The Shape of Sola Scriptura*: "[Many in] the medieval church interpreted the 'rock' as Peter's faith, not Peter himself."

Dwight: I haven't read Mathison's book, but the title makes me wonder if he might be a bit biased. He's right that Catholics share with Protestants the belief that the *rock* in this verse refers to Peter's rock-like confession. However, he is incorrect in saying that Catholics do not also seen the rock as referring to Peter. I could quote a number of Catholic writers in support of this view, but one will suffice. Writing around the year 220, the great North African theologian Tertullian said, "The Lord said to Peter, 'On this rock I will build my church. I have given you the keys of the kingdom of heaven [and] upon you I will build my church.'"

Catholic commentators down through the ages have seen the rock as being both the confession *and* the man Peter. The

Catechism of the Catholic Church puts it this way: "Because of the faith he confessed, Peter will remain the unshakeable rock of the church" (Article 552). For Catholics, the meaning of Matthew 16:18 is that Jesus intended to build his church on Simon Peter.

John: Catholics put an enormous amount of weight on Matthew 16:17-19 as the basis for their belief that Peter was the representative of Christ on earth, and that he passed this authority on to successor bishops of Rome. This has led some to refer to Catholics as 'Matthew Christians.'

Dwight: We don't draw the founding role of Peter from these verses alone. Another important passage comes from the last chapter of John's Gospel, where Jesus says to Peter, "Feed my lambs ... Tend my sheep ... Feed my sheep" (John 21:15-19). In these passages, Jesus, the good shepherd, is passing his pastoral authority on to Peter. These verses corroborate and support those in Matthew.

In Catholicism, Peter is referred to as the 'chief of the apostles' and the first bishop of Rome (papal reign: 30-67). This, however, seems like a reading back into history. Catholic historian D. W. O'Connor, in his book *Peter in Rome*, says the belief that "Peter founded the church in Rome is extremely doubtful, and [the claim] that he served as its first bishop for even one year is an unfounded tradition that can be traced back to a point no earlier than the third century."

John: What is the historical evidence for the belief that Peter was the first bishop of Rome, given the opinion of O'Connor and others that Peter was not the founder or unquestioned leader of the Roman church? Doing so appears to be a fiction—maybe an important fiction, because of Peter's prominence in the Gospels as the spokesperson for the disciples—but a fiction nonetheless.

Dwight: O'Connor states the accepted Catholic position. We don't pretend that Peter founded the church in Rome or that he was its unquestioned leader during his lifetime. But it is almost certain that he was one of the leaders of the Roman church, and the evidence that he was martyred in Rome is both early and well substantiated.

The New Testament is sketchy about the activities of the apostles after Pentecost. We can piece together some of Peter's missionary travels. We know that after the Jewish persecution of Christians broke out in Jerusalem, Peter fled (Acts 12:17). We know that he ministered in Antioch (Galatians 2:11-21), most likely in the years 40-41, and that Antioch was probably his mission base, as it was for Paul. And it appears from his first letter that Peter may have traveled through Pontus, Asia, Galatia, Cappadocia and Bithynia (1 Peter 1:1). At the end of his first letter, Peter mentions that he is writing from Babylon, a code word among early Christians for Rome, which indicates that he lived out his final years in Rome. According to tradition, Peter was crucified upside down, saying that he was not worthy to be crucified like Christ.

Being the most prominent of Jesus' followers, to whom Jesus said, "Feed my sheep" (John 21:15-17), it is reasonable to conclude that Peter had a senior position in the Roman church. Ignatius of Antioch, who probably knew Peter, said that he was not only the leader of the Roman church, but of the church universal. For the first 1,500 years of Christianity, Peter's leadership of the church was never doubted.

John: In John's Gospel, Jesus says that he will send the Holy Spirit "to teach you all things" (John 14:26) and "to guide you into all truth" (John 16:13), which came upon the disciples and others on the first Pentecost after Jesus' ascension, as recorded in Acts 2:1-13. This seems to imply that the one who would assure the faithful preservation and proclamation of the truth is the Holy Spirit, not the bishop of Rome.

Dwight: Does it have to be 'either-or'? The Holy Spirit assures the faith, but the Holy Spirit works through real people. Jesus gave Peter the mission to confirm his brothers in the faith (Luke 22:32), and he was the leader of the apostles on the day of Pentecost when the Holy Spirit came upon Jesus' followers in Jerusalem. We believe that Peter and successive bishops of Rome were baptized with the power of the Holy Spirit. They defined and defended the faith from the very beginning, and do so today, and will continue doing so in the years ahead.

John: If the pope is the 'supreme pontiff' of Christ's church, as Catholics claim, what about active, believing Protestant and Eastern Orthodox Christians who do not accept the supremacy of the pope?

Dwight: The Catholic Church, especially since Vatican II, recognizes as brothers and sisters in the faith all who are baptized and profess faith in Jesus Christ. The body of Christ would be stronger if we were one unified church; also, we could learn from one another. Catholics, for instance, could learn much from Protestants about scripture reading and Bible study, and also about evangelism and mission work.

In defense of the papal office, some Catholics say that it assures a unified position on issues related to faith and morals, but some papal teachings are not followed. In 1968, Pope Paul VI issued an encyclical (circular letter) against the use of artificial means of contraception, *Humanae Vitae* (*On Human Life*), that taught that every sexual act must have the potential for the creation of human life. Polls indicate that the vast majority of American Catholics do not agree with the pope's encyclical against the use of birth control.

Dwight: The Catholic Church doesn't teach what it thinks people want to hear or what they will obey. It teaches what it believes to be the truth, because it is the *truth*. We don't change or amend the Ten Commandments because some people are not able to keep them.

Catholic teaching is consistent, clear, unified and complete, both doctrinally and morally. Yes, some Catholics dissent from the Church's teachings, but what church experiences full obedience from all its members? Failures do not nullify the truth of what the Catholic Church teaches. Catholics may disagree with the Church's teachings on artificial contraception, but this does not invalidate the teachings; truth is not determined by majority vote.

Apostolic Succession: From the First Century to the Twenty-first. Jesus said, "As the Father has sent me, so I am sending you" (John 20:21). This *sending* underlies the doctrine of apostolic succession, the teaching that Catholic bishops stand in an unbroken line back to Jesus' original apostles, whom he called to "make disciples of all nations [all *peoples*], baptizing them ... and teaching them to obey everything I have commanded you" (Matthew 28:19-20). Catholics believe that 'apostolic succession' is a divine institution, guarded by the Holy Spirit, to guarantee an authentic, back-to-the-apostles witness to the truth. It is transmitted through the laying on of hands in the consecration of bishops. The Orthodox Church also believes in apostolic succession, as do Anglicans/Episcopalians, though the latter call it the Historic Episcopacy and have a different understanding of its nature. For most Protestants, 'apostolic' refers to the teachings of the apostles that are recorded in the books of the New Testament, rather than a mechanical, unbroken succession of bishops from the first century to the present day.

John: Catholics claim that 'apostolic succession' assures the faithful passing on of the apostolic witness to Jesus' life and teachings. Isn't this witness more carefully preserved and transmitted through the Gospels and other books in the New Testament, the *written* apostolic testimony to Jesus?

Dwight: Again, it is not a question of either-or. We believe fully in the apostolic witness of the Gospels; it is the apostolic succession that makes this witness a living, dynamic truth. As we saw in Chaper 3, Catholics believe many of the same things that Protestants believe, but we affirm more than Protestants do. We believe in the apostolic authority of the Gospels, but we also affirm the apostolic authority of the church, which comes both from scripture and the early church fathers.

The belief that the early church leaders were the successors of the apostles is one of the foundational truths of Catholicism. Irenaeus, the bishop of Lyons, who was taught by Polycarp, the bishop of Smyrna, who had been taught by the apostle John, said, "We appeal again to that tradition which is derived from the apostles and safeguarded in the churches through the succession of presbyters."

John: As to the succession itself, if there were no *bishops* until the end of the first century, as many church historians, even Catholic historians, believe, how can the Catholic Church claim that there has been an unbroken line of bishops from Peter to the present day? This seems, again, like a fiction—maybe an important fiction, but a fiction nonetheless.

Dwight: I am not sure what you mean when you say there were no bishops until the end of the first century. Maybe these men were not called 'bishops' at the beginning, but call them what you will, they believed they had inherited their apostolic authority from the apostles, as seen in a letter by Clement, the third bishop of Rome, dated in the year 96, to the church in Corinth.

Apostolic succession is not a second or third-century belief; it goes back to the very beginning of the church. Tertullian, the North African scholar referred to above, writing around the year 200, said, "But if any are bold enough to insert themselves into the apostolic age ... let them unroll their list of bishops in unbroken succession from the beginning." I could quote authority after authority to show that apostolic succession was part and parcel of the church's early history.

Papal Infallibility: Without Error. Catholics believe that the pope is infallible when he speaks *ex cathedra* on matters of faith and morals. The Catholic Church does not claim that the pope *himself* is infallible—a common misunderstanding—only his pronouncements, and only when speaking on matters of faith and morals. The term *ex cathedra* comes from a Latin word for throne or chair, from which we also get the word *cathedral*, the building that houses the bishop's chair. The term goes back to Roman days when emperors sat on a throne or chair and made public pronouncements. It goes even farther back in Jewish tradition to the 'chair of Moses,' the seat that Jewish authorities sat on to pronounce judgments and interpretations of the law (see Exodus 18:13 and Matthew 23:2). The belief in papal infallibility goes back to the thirteenth century; it was made Catholic dogma in 1870.

When the bishop of Rome speaks *ex cathedra*—from the bishop's chair in Saint Peter's Basilica—his pronouncements on matters of faith and morals are deemed to be infallible, that is, without error. When the pope speaks in this regard, he is not doing so as an individual but as the vicar of Christ, the one authorized to speak corporately for and on behalf of the church. Papal pronouncements are not deemed infallible when the pope speaks about non-faith matters, for instance, about history, economics, science, politics and the like. The two most recent papal *ex cathedra* pronouncements had to do with Mary: that she was conceived immaculate, which was declared Catholic dogma in 1854, and that she was bodily assumed into heaven upon her death, which was declared dogma in 1950.

The basis for the Catholic Church's belief in papal infallibility is twofold. First, Catholicism understands Matthew 16:18-19 and John 21:15-17 as referring to Christ's commissioning Peter to lead the church, and to pass this authority along to his successors. Second, it believes that the Holy Spirit protects the pope, as the leader of the church, from error when speaking about faith and morals. Thus the belief that the pope's pronouncements are without error requires the further belief that the Holy Spirit watches over the pope when he speaks *ex cathedra*.

Protestants understand Jesus' words, "You are Peter, and on this rock I will build my church … and I will give you the keys of the kingdom" (Matthew 16:18-19) may have to do with the founding and initial leadership of the church, but they don't read them as having anything to do with papal 'infallibility.'

John: What is the basis for the belief that the pope is infallible when he speaks *ex cathedra*?

Dwight: Strictly speaking, it is only Christ who is infallible, but he grants a measure of his infallibility to the Church. The pope, as the vicar or corporate representative of Christ on earth and the supreme pontiff of the Catholic Church, has, in this capacity, a special but limited measure of infallibility.

John: If the pope is considered infallible in the area of faith and morals, I can see how some Catholics might believe that papal pronouncements about other matters are infallible as well. Does this, in fact, happen?

Dwight: I suppose some Catholics might consider every papal pronouncement infallible. For me, questions concerning infallibility—whether a particular teaching is infallible, or maybe just a little bit infallible, or perhaps not infallible at all—miss the point. We are called to obey Christ's teachings, as understood and interpreted by the Church, with an open, willing heart.

MARY
The Mother of God

It is said that Mary is the 'face' of Catholicism. She is venerated, not worshipped, as some Protestants mistakenly believe, as *Theokotos*, a Greek term meaning 'God-bearer.' This title was accorded Mary at the Council of Ephesus in 431, because she gave birth to the Son of God. Mary is also called the 'Mother of God,' because she was Jesus' mother and Jesus was God-incarnate. Initially, the term emphasized the divine nature of the *Son* of Mary; later, at least in Catholicism, the emphasis changed to the *mother* of the Son, that is, to Mary herself. The New Testament, in referring to Mary, never uses the term Mother of God because God, as to his divine nature, did not have a 'mother.' Although Mary is the most important woman in the history of the Church, very little is known about her, other than she was very young when she conceived—probably thirteen or fourteen, much younger than the matronly Mary we are used to seeing in Christian art—a virgin, the cousin of Elizabeth, and that she found favor with God and was chosen to bear his Son.

Mary is the second Eve—in medieval art, Mary is often pictured holding an apple—the one who obeyed God, saying, "Let it be with me according to your word" (Luke 1:38). Catholics believe that Mary was assumed bodily into heaven and, just as Jesus 'sits' at the right hand of God (Hebrews 1:3), she sits at the right hand of Jesus. Mary used to be called a *co-redemptrix*, suggesting that she had a role in the work of redemption. This term is no longer used; Vatican II thought that it confused Jesus' exclusive role in the work of salvation. Some Protestants say that Catholics take Mary too seriously. Catholics say that Protestants don't take her seriously enough, that is, do not accord her sufficient honor and praise as the mother of our Lord, though this is changing in many Protestant denominations.

There are two passages that seem at odds with the Catholic understanding of the special place or role of Mary. In Mark 3:33-35, Jesus is traveling through Galilee and stops at a house. Someone outside the house says to him, "Your mother and your brothers and sisters are outside, asking for you." Jesus responds, not acknowledging Mary but saying, instead, "Whoever does the will of God is my brother and sister and mother." In Luke 11:27-28, Jesus is on his way to Jerusalem. Along the way someone says to him, "Blessed is the womb that bore you and the breasts that nursed you." Jesus answers, again not acknowledging Mary, saying, "Blessed rather are those who hear the word of God and obey it." Catholics say that Jesus is not here disavowing Mary; rather, he is extending his 'family' to include those who hear, follow and obey the word of God.

Outside the infancy narratives in Matthew (1:18-2:23) and Luke (1:26-2:52), Mary is hardly mentioned by name in the Gospels; in fact, she is named only two times, not counting duplications, though in John's Gospel she is referred to as Jesus' 'mother' at the wedding at Cana and at the foot of the cross. Paul does not mention Mary by name in any of his thirteen letters, nor does John in his three letters, nor Peter in his two letters—which is not surprising because Peter, Paul and John rarely mention the names of *any* people in their writings.

John: In your book on Mary, you said, "One of the final obstacles to becoming a Catholic was the problem of Mary." What did you mean by "the problem of Mary"? How did you overcome the *problem*?

Dwight: In my Protestant childhood I was taught that Mary was the Catholic Church's biggest error. In becoming a Catholic, I had to re-examine my understandable prejudice in this matter and think again. The problem was with me, not with Mary or the Catholic Church. Over a number of years, as an Anglican, I pondered the Marian teachings and eventually came to accept them. During this time I began to use the rosary and the Holy

Spirit led me to a deeper understanding of the incarnation and into a deeper love for the Lord through this ancient, widespread practice, which properly venerates Mary as the mother of Christ.

Mary's Sinlessness: The Immaculate Conception. The immaculate conception is the belief that Mary was conceived *immaculate*, that is, with no taint or stain of original sin. It refers to Mary's conception, not that of Jesus. (Jesus' conception is referred to as the 'virginal conception.') The reason for this teaching seems to have been the church's felt-need to answer those who asked, "If all humans are sinful, because of Adam's sin, how can Jesus, who was born of Mary and inherited her flesh, be sinless?" The Catholic Church's answer is that Mary was born immaculate through a special dispensation of God's grace, which preserved her from original sin. Protestants say that there are several references to Jesus' sinlessness in the New Testament—"God made him who had no sin" (2 Corinthians 5:21); "in him there was no sin" (1 John 3:5); "yet he was without sin" (Hebrews 4:15)—but nowhere is it said, written or claimed that Mary was sinless.

The belief in Mary's sinlessness goes back to the early church. The first person to champion Mary's immaculate conception was John Duns Scotus in the late 1200s. The matter was left undecided at the Council of Trent (mid-1500s); it was made dogma by Pope Pius IX in 1854. (Mary's immaculate conception was the first dogma of the church that was defined by a pope without the concurrence of a church council.) For the most part, the Protestant Reformers rejected the teaching, because they considered the claim that Mary was sinless to be contrary to the biblical teaching that "all have sinned" (Romans 3:23). The Reformers believed that because Jesus was the Son of God, he was, by this very fact, sinless.

Catholics, in defending Mary's immaculate conception, look to Luke 1:28, in which the angel Gabriel says to Mary, "Greetings, favored one. The Lord is with you." Protestants understand the word *favored* in Luke 1:28 to mean that Mary was the one favored to bear God's Son. Catholics say that the original meaning of the word 'favored' meant 'full of grace,' and to be full of grace means to be without sin. Catholics admit that the formal doctrine of Mary's immaculate conception developed over time; but, they say, so did the belief in the Trinity, which likewise is not found, at least literally, in the Bible. Protestants say there is a difference between the two, however, because there is underlying scriptural support for the doctrine of the Trinity, two examples being Matthew 28:19 ("and of the Father and of the Son and of the Holy Spirit") and 2 Corinthians 13:14. There are no verses or scriptural texts to support the claim that Mary was conceived without sin.

The place one would expect to find scriptural support for Mary's immaculate conception would be Luke's infancy narrative, which is told from Mary's perspective. There is nothing in the Lukan narrative to suggest that Mary was conceived *immaculate* or that she was in any way sinless. Though this may be, Catholics point out that Mary was highly honored in the first century, and from the mid-second century on it was widely held that she was the 'all holy,' pure, spotless vessel for God's incarnate son.

Although Mary's immaculate conception was widely believed in both the Eastern and Western Churches, it took almost nineteen centuries (until 1854) for it to become Catholic dogma. One reason may be that there were objections from Catholic scholars and theologians, including both Augustine and Aquinas, because sin is endemic to the human condition. Notwithstanding certain objections, Mary's sinlessness is now Catholic dogma; it was only after the Reformation that anyone began to seriously question this belief.

John: Catholic teaching about Mary's immaculate conception seems at odds with Paul's statement that "all have sinned and fall short of the glory of God" (Romans 3:23). Was this done to honor Mary as the mother of God?

Dwight: If Jesus was true God and true Man, then he was sinless. This would have been impossible if he were born of a sinful woman, since he would have inherited original sin from her. The Catholic Church concluded that for Jesus to have been sinless, his mother, from whom he took his human nature, must also have been sinless, which came from a special grace of God. If our readers want to know more about Mary's immaculate conception, as well as other Marian beliefs and doctrines, I recommend that they read my book *Mary: A Catholic/Evangelical Debate.*

Mary's Perpetual Virginity: Before, During and After. Catholics believe that Mary was a virgin before, during (that is, Mary's hymen was not broken during delivery) and after Jesus' birth. We tend to think of virginity in sexual terms; the early church saw Mary's virginity as a sign of innocence to keep pure the womb that bore the Son of God.

One problem with the Catholic belief that Mary was a perpetual virgin is that there are multiple references to Jesus' brothers (really, *half*-brothers) in the New Testament: Mark 3:31 ("his mother and *brothers*"); Mark 6:1-3, in which the people of Nazareth, who had known Jesus and his family from childhood, refer to Jesus' four brothers by name and mention that he also had sisters (these verses are repeated in Matthew 13:55); John 2:12 ("with his mother, his *brothers* and his disciples"); John 7:3 ("his *brothers*"); Acts 1:14 ("Mary, the mother of Jesus, as well as his *brothers*"); and Galatians 1:19 ("James, the Lord's *brother*"). These textual references indicate that Matthew, Mark, Luke, John and Paul understood Jesus' 'brothers' as *blood* brothers, rather than as *step*brothers.

Jerome, the great linguist, taught that Jesus' brothers and sisters were his cousins; others, especially in the Eastern Church, said that Jesus' brothers and sisters were children of Joseph from a previous marriage. Protestant scholars argue that Jesus' brothers and sisters could not have been his cousins, because the New Testament, in referring to Jesus' brothers and sisters, uses the normal Greek word for brother (*adelphos*), rather than the Greek word for cousin (*anepsios*), which we find in Colossians 4:10, where Paul mentions that Mark was "the cousin of Barnabas." Catholics point out that in the *Septuagint*, the Greek word *adelphos* is also used to refer to cousins, nephews and uncles, that is, one's kinsmen; it does not mean *only* 'brother.' Furthermore, Catholics say that nowhere in the New Testament can it be shown that Mary was the *actual* mother of Jesus' so-called siblings. Doing so, they say, is offering an argument from silence.

One text the Catholic Church uses to support its claim that Jesus had no biological brothers or sisters is Jesus' statement from the cross in John's Gospel, in which he tells "the disciple whom he loved" (presumably John, though the text does not say this) from the cross to care for Mary as he would his very own mother (John 19:26-27). The Protestant understanding of these verses is quite different. John's Gospel says that "even [Jesus'] brothers did not believe in him" (John 7:5) and, like the other disciples, had probably fled in fear following Jesus' arrest (Matthew 26:56b), so Jesus asked the one who was with him at Calvary to care for his mother.

John: Who are the four named 'brothers' of Jesus in Mark 6:3? Are they Jesus' stepbrothers, or cousins, or Joseph's sons from a previous marriage? The principal reason for the claim that Jesus had no biological siblings, it seems, was to honor and preserve Mary's special status as the mother of our Lord.

Dwight: We don't know who Jesus' step-siblings were, for sure; Catholic opinion is divided. We simply say they were Jesus' 'kinsmen,' which can mean either children of Joseph from a previous marriage or Jesus' cousins. There were extended families in the first century and terms were not precise. Personally, I believe that Jesus' stepbrothers and stepsisters were his 'kinsmen.'

Regarding Mary's virginity, the Catholic Church has the weight of tradition on its side: for 1,500 years the perpetual virginity of Mary was accepted by Christians in both the East and West. Luther and Calvin accepted Mary's virginity, and even some who came after them, like the Wesleys. From a Catholic point of view, the denial of Mary's perpetual virginity is a very late invention.

Another argument that is sometimes raised against the claim that Mary remained a virgin is that, in first-century Judaism, for Mary to have denied Joseph his conjugal rights would have been a direct violation of the marriage covenant, and Joseph and Mary were clearly man and wife, as set forth in Jesus' genealogy in Matthew's Gospel: "Joseph, the *husband* of Mary, of whom was born Jesus" (Matthew 1:16). Matthew goes on to record that Joseph "had no marital relations [with Mary] *until* she had borne a son" (1:25). Catholics read this verse to mean, and only mean, that Jesus was not the son of Joseph—that is, that Joseph was not Jesus' *father*. A more natural reading of 'until,' however, is that after Jesus' birth, Joseph and Mary *had* sexual relations. Catholics respond that the Greek word for *until* (*hoes*) does not imply a change of circumstances (before and after), as does the English word 'until.'

The Protestant Reformers were not concerned about Mary's perpetual virginity. Most read the New Testament references to Jesus' brothers and sisters as being the children of Joseph and Mary. For the Reformers, the important point was not Mary's virginity or Jesus' virgin birth but Jesus' virginal conception: he was conceived apart from a human father, that is, *supernaturally*, by God himself, through the agency and power of the Holy Spirit (Luke 1:35).

John: I am not sure what 'virgin birth' means. Does it mean that Jesus did not pass through the birth canal, that is, that Mary's hymen was not ruptured?

Dwight: The Catholic Church, in faithfulness to traditions that go back to the beginning of the church, teaches that Mary remained a virgin before, through and after the birth of Christ, that is, the physical birth of Jesus did not destroy her virginity. Whether this means the hymen was or was not ruptured, I honestly don't know, but clearly Jesus' birth was a vaginal birth. My answer is not part of any 'Mary honoring' agenda. I am simply following the church's teaching, going back to Jerome and Ambrose in the fourth century, that Mary was and remained a virgin.

Mary's Assumption into Heaven: At the Right Hand of Jesus. The Catholic Church believes that shortly after Mary's death, her body and soul were assumed into heaven, where she now resides with Jesus. (It is said that Mary gave Jesus bodily life on earth, and that he gave her bodily life in heaven.) The support for Mary's assumption is sparse, which even Catholic scholars admit, though it seems to have been believed as early as the sixth century; in the seventh century, Mary's assumption became a feast day (August 15). Mary's bodily assumption became official Catholic dogma as a result of Pope Pius XII's *ex cathedra* declaration in 1950.

There is some confusion between the words *ascension* and *assumption*. Jesus' ascension is mentioned at the end of Luke's Gospel (24:50-51) and at the beginning of the book of Acts (1:9-11). Jesus ascended to heaven by his own power. In Catholic theology, Mary was assumed body and soul into heaven by the power of God; because she was sinless, she did not have to pass through purgatory.

The first written account of Mary being assumed bodily into heaven goes back to John of Damascus in the eighth century. He said that Mary died in the presence of all of the apostles, but when they opened her grave, it was empty.

There is some disagreement about whether Mary died and then was raised and went to heaven (John of Damascus), or went straight to heaven from earth like Elijah in 2 Kings 2:11. There is further confusion about the place from which Mary was 'assumed.' Some believe that it was Ephesus, where the apostle John lived until the end of the first century, because of Mary's association with John after Jesus' departure ("And from that hour the disciple took her into his own home," John 19:27b). Others, like John of Damascus, believe that she was assumed from Jerusalem.

Because Mary is in heaven, she is sometimes called the Queen of Heaven. This belief comes from both scripture and tradition. Catholics identify the woman crowned with the sun in Revelation 12 as Mary, which certainly is a possible interpretation because the woman is clearly the mother of Jesus. Some Catholics also appeal to Matthew's statement that the tombs were open and "many bodies of the saints who had fallen to sleep were raised" (Matthew 27:52). This, however, is a dubious interpretation, because the text only says that some were raised, and it doesn't refer to Mary, and it says nothing about ascending to heaven.

As with Mary's immaculate conception and perpetual virginity, there is no scriptural support for the claim that she was assumed into heaven upon or after her earthly death. Catholics claim that because there is no grave identified as that of Mary, and there are no reports of Marian physical relics being preserved, she must have been assumed into heaven, but this is an argument from silence. Further, one has to wonder why it took two thousand years (until 1950) for Mary's assumption to become *de fide* ('must-be-believed') Catholic dogma. Catholics reply that the belief that Mary was assumed into heaven, though only *formally* defined as dogma in 1950, goes back to the mid-first millennium.

John: It is clear that Mary is very esteemed in Catholicism. In fact, it almost seems like Catholics pray more to Mary than they do to Jesus, as in the rosary, and that the Catholic Church encourages this. Is this correct?

Dwight: Catholics do offer prayers *to* Mary, just as they do to the saints, but they worship *only* God. I can understand, though, how some might think that Catholics "pray more to Mary than they do to Jesus." What non-Catholics miss is the centrality of the Mass for Catholics. The Mass is totally and completely focused on Jesus Christ and his death on the cross. Look at Catholic churches: the altar and the crucifix are central; Mary is always in a side chapel, which is emblematic of the relationship between Jesus and Mary. Our most recent popes, John XXIII, Paul VI and John Paul II, all emphasized that devotion to Mary is secondary to the worship to be given to her son.

Catholics pray to Mary and the saints because they are closer to Jesus than we are. We pray *to* Mary to pray *for* us, just as we would ask someone who was a prayer partner to pray for us. For Catholics, Mary is a powerful intercessor because she is the mother of our risen, reigning Lord and Savior.

Protestants often challenge Catholics on their Marian beliefs and practices, but I think it is fair for Catholics to challenge Protestants as well. You wonder why we venerate Mary so highly and pray to her so much; we wonder why you don't. At the cross, Jesus said to 'the disciple whom he loved,' and therefore to us, "Here is your mother" (John 19:27). In Luke 1, the angel Gabriel honored Mary; Elizabeth, the mother of John the Baptist, honored Mary; the unborn John the Baptist honored Mary when he lept in her womb; and Mary herself said, "From now on all generations will call me blessed" (Luke 1:48). The majority of Christians down through the ages, in both Eastern and Western Churches, have honored Mary as the mother of our Lord.

The pope and Mary are central to Catholicism. Another important aspect is the sacraments. Protestants and Catholics both observe the sacraments of baptism and Holy Communion, though they understand them differently. In addition, Catholics view as sacraments confirmation, reconciliation, matrimony, holy orders and anointing the sick. We will look at all seven sacraments in the next chapter.

CHAPTER SIX

The Sacraments

Mystery, Meaning and Mumbo Jumbo

The Episcopal Church is a sacramental church, so I was familiar with baptism and Holy Communion, and I assumed that confirmation was a sacrament because the Episcopal bishop of Minnesota laid hands on and 'confirmed' me in 1946. The word sacrament comes from the Latin *sacramentum*, meaning 'sacred oath,' referring to oaths that Roman soldiers took in which they pledged their lives to the emperor. Tertullian applied the word to baptism as a rite in which one pledged his or her life to Christ.

THE SACRAMENTS
Means of Grace or Symbols of Grace?

Sacraments are understood by sacramental churches as ritual acts that manifest and bestow God's grace upon believers. In the words of the *Book of Common Prayer*, sacraments are "an outward and visible sign of an inward and spiritual grace." The Belgian Dominican Edward Schillebeeckx said that just as we encounter God in the tangible person of Jesus, so we encounter Jesus in the tangible sacraments. Non-sacramental Protestant churches view the sacraments symbolically, and prefer the word 'ordinance' to sacrament, meaning that Christ *ordained* these acts. The sacraments are the heart and soul of Catholicism, the most distinguishing mark of what it means to be Catholic.

There are three major differences between Protestants and Catholics regarding the sacraments. First, Catholics have a sevenfold sacramental system, and they believe that Jesus instituted all seven. Protestants believe that Jesus instituted only two sacraments, baptism and Holy Communion. Second, Catholics believe that the sacraments are efficacious, that is, they impart or convey God's grace. The technical term for this is *ex opera operato*, meaning 'from the performance of the act itself.' Few Protestants would agree with this. Third, Catholics believe that observing the sacraments is necessary for salvation, as set forth in Chapter 4. Protestants do not regard the sacraments as essential for salvation.

John: As I understand, based on my reading of the *Catechism of the Catholic Church*, Catholics believe that faith, to be saving faith, must be accompanied by regular observance of the sacraments. If observing the sacraments is necessary for salvation, and the church is the channel through which the sacraments are made available, would it be fair to say that Catholics are dependent on the church for their salvation?

Dwight: Like our Protestant brothers and sisters, we believe that we are dependent on Jesus Christ for our salvation. Where do we find Christ alive in the world today? In the church, which the apostle Paul calls the body of Christ. The church is the vehicle of salvation because the church administers the sacraments, which are the means of salvation.

THE GOSPEL SACRAMENTS
Baptism and Communion

The number of sacraments in Protestantism is two: baptism and Holy Communion. Protestants sometimes call these the Gospel Sacraments, because they were instituted by Jesus when he told his disciples, "Go and make disciples of all nations, *baptizing* them in the name of … " (Matthew 28:19); and at the Last Supper when he told his disciples, in breaking the bread and drinking the wine, "*Do this* in remembrance of me" (Luke 22:19). Protestants and Catholics agree on the Gospel Sacraments, but have different understandings as to their meaning and efficacy.

Sacramental grace, which flows through the sacraments, is directly proportional to the faith of the recipient. If one comes to the Lord's Table, for instance, with no faith, the sacrament of Holy Eucharist or Holy Communion has no power.

Baptism: "In the Name of the Father, the Son and the Holy Spirit." Historically, sacramental Protestants have understood baptism as the way one enters the family of God, as circumcision was for Jewish males in ancient Israel—though churches that practice 'believer's baptism' would not agree, because circumcision is for infants and they do not baptize infants. Infants are not baptized on the basis of *their* faith, but on the faith of their sponsors (parents or godparents) and that of the church.

In Catholicism, the rite of baptism used to be called 'christening,' emphasizing that this was the way one became a Christian. This term is not often used today. Catholics believe that baptism is essential for salvation, as set forth in the *Catechism of the Catholic Church* (Article 1257). In Catholicism, grace is conferred in baptism *ex opera operato* and washes away the taint or stain of original sin. For most Protestants, baptism is unrelated to original sin; it is understood, rather, as a sign or symbol of one's new life in Christ.

Adult baptism was practiced in the first-century church, based on Peter's words to the crowd in Jerusalem on the first Pentecost: "Repent and be baptized ... in the name of Jesus Christ ... so that your sins may be forgiven" (Acts 2:38-39). In the second century, Christians began to baptize infants and children, as well as adults. A practical reason for this was the high rate of infant mortality: parents did not want their unbaptized children to die with original sin on their souls.

In some Protestant denominations infants are *dedicated* rather than baptized. Baptism for such persons is delayed until they are able to make a conscious decision for Christ. Baptism is also delayed in Baptist, Brethren and denominations that practice 'believer's baptism.' In these denominations, baptism follows one's public profession of faith, after which the candidate is immersed three times (in the name of the Father, the Son and the Holy Spirit). Immersion was the baptismal practice in the early church (the word *baptize* means 'to immerse'). Today, in most mainline Protestant churches, and also Catholic churches, water is sprinkled ('aspersion') or poured ('affusion') three times over an infant's or an adult's head.

John: If an unbaptized person cannot go to heaven, what about Quakers and those in the Salvation Army, who are Christians to be sure, but do not believe in baptism—or, in fact, any of the sacraments?

Dwight: The Catholic Church believes in the 'baptism of desire.' This means that if a person understands what baptism means and has the opportunity to be baptized, but cannot because there is no priest to administer the sacrament, as was the case in Japan in the 1600s when Catholic priests were driven out of the country, the believer would not be denied salvation because he or she had not been baptized. As for Christians who do not believe in or practice baptism, we leave this to God's mercy.

John: If unbaptized persons cannot go to heaven because Adam's sin has not been removed, what about unbaptized infants? Are they lost forever? There used to be an escape clause called *limbo*, from the Latin *limbus* ('border'), a place of eternal peace, but not heaven itself. I understand that today limbo is not part of the Catholic Church's catechism, nor is it a denied belief.

Dwight: The Catholic Church has never formally included 'limbo' as *de fide* doctrine. The concept goes back to the early church, which worried about the fate of unbaptized infants. Again, we leave the eternal state of those who have not been baptized—those who die in infancy, pagans who have never heard the good news, Christians from traditions that do not baptize—to God's overwhelming justice and mercy.

Holy Communion: "Do This in Remembrance of Me." Boston College professor of philosophy Peter Kreeft said, "The sacraments are the crown of the Catholic Church, and the Eucharist is the crown of the sacraments." For Catholics, the Eucharist is clearly the most important sacrament, and the only *repeatable* sacrament, other than confession/reconciliation. The other sacraments—baptism, confirmation, matrimony, holy orders and anointing the sick—are mostly one-time-only sacraments.

One difference between Protestants and Catholics regarding Eucharist/Communion is its importance and centrality in worship. Holy Eucharist is central to Catholic worship; in Protestantism, the center of worship is the sermon—the preaching of God's truth from God's word. Though Communion is observed each Sunday in Episcopal, Lutheran and other sacramental churches, in Presbyterian, Methodist, Congregational and many other churches it is celebrated only once a month, and in some churches, only once a quarter.

There are various names or terms for this sacrament. The most common terms in Protestantism are the *Lord's Supper,* referring to the meal that Jesus celebrated with his disciples on the evening before his death (the term 'Lord's Supper' comes from 1 Corinthians 11:20), and *Holy Communion,* referring to the 'common union' communicants have with one another in the celebration of the Lord's Supper. The name for the sacrament in Catholicism is *Holy Eucharist,* which comes from the Greek word for 'thanksgiving,' referring to Jesus giving 'thanks' over the bread and wine at the Last Supper (Luke 22:17-19). The Catholic worship service at which Holy Eucharist is celebrated is called the *Mass,* from the Latin *misso,* meaning 'to dismiss,' referring to the early church's practice of dismissing catechumens (adult converts who had not yet been baptized into the church) before the celebration of the Eucharist. Today it refers to the priest's words of dismissal at the end of the service: "The Mass is ended. Go in peace."

Catholics believe that Christ is sacramentally present in the bread and wine. The term used to describe this is *transubstantiation*, referring to the *trans*formation of the bread and wine—the substances—into the 'real presence' of Christ's body and blood. Transubstantiation does not explain *how* the change takes place, only *what* changes, that is, the 'substances.' The elements may look, smell and taste like bread and wine, but when they are consecrated they become the actual body and blood of Christ.

The transubstantiation of the elements occurs when the celebrating priest pronounces the words of consecration: "Take, eat, this is my body … Take, drink, this is my blood," which come from Jesus' words at the Last Supper (as in Matthew 26:26-29). Most Protestants believe that Christ is present in the *celebration* of the Lord's Supper, but not *physically* present in the elements themselves. Non-sacramental Protestants regard the Lord's Supper as a memorial ("Do this in *remembrance* of me," Luke 22:19b).

John: Jesus said to his disciples, "This is my body, which is given for you … This cup is the new covenant in my blood, which is poured out for you" (Luke 22:19-20). Most Protestants understand these words symbolically, because Jesus was sitting amongst the disciples. He was not offering his *actual* body and blood; he was saying that the elements *represented* his body and blood. This seems like the most natural reading of Jesus' words.

Dwight: Catholics believe that Jesus meant the elements to be understood as his *actual* body and blood, based on his words to the crowds following the feeding of the five thousand on the shore of the Sea of Galilee in the Gospel of John, when he said, "Those who eat my flesh and drink my blood have eternal life" (John 6:54). At the Last Supper, it is doubtful that the disciples thought they were eating Jesus' body and drinking his blood;

this only became clear after his death on the cross. Looking back, they understood the Last Supper as a ritual meal that brought Jesus' body-and-blood sacrifice into the present, much like the Passover *seder* brings the Israelites' exodus from Egypt into the present.

John: I don't understand the connection between the Passover meal and the Last Supper. Both, it seems to me, are meant to be understood *symbolically*. The food eaten at Passover meals, even today, symbolizes the Jews' bitter plight in Egypt before God saved them with "a mighty hand and an outstretched arm" (Deuteronomy 4:34). The Last Supper looked ahead to Jesus' sacrificial offering on the cross. The bread and wine symbolize Jesus' death for the sins of the world ("This is my body, which is given for you … This cup is the new covenant in my blood," Luke 22:19-20). In the case of Passover, the 'meal items' are understood symbolically. For me, the same is true of the meal items at the Last Supper.

Most Protestants understand the bread-body, wine-blood language as similar to Jesus' "I am" statements in John's Gospel. Protestant scholars Norman Geisler and Ralph MacKenzie, in their book *Roman Catholics and Evangelicals*, point out that when Jesus said, "I am the light of the world" (John 8:12), he did not mean that he was actually a light; when he said, "I am the gate" (John 10:9), he did not mean that he was a literal gate; when he said, "I am the true vine" (John 15:1), he did not mean that he was an actual vine. Likewise, when he said, "This is my body … this is my blood," he was not saying that the bread and wine *were* his body and blood; rather, he meant that they *represented* his body and blood.

John: I have never understood how Catholics can read Jesus' words at the Last Supper so literally. On what basis do you differentiate these words from sayings that are meant to be understood symbolically, like Jesus' "I am" sayings?

Dwight: Jesus said, "Unless you eat the flesh of the Son of Man and drink his blood, you have no life in you" (John 6:54). After saying this, "many of his disciples turned back and no longer went about with him" because it was a "difficult" teaching. He did not call them back and say, "You misunderstood me. I was only speaking symbolically." Instead, he asked who else would leave him because they could not accept this saying.

It would be much easier, of course, to accept the popular mainline Protestant understanding of the Eucharist—that Jesus' body-blood words are to be understood symbolically rather than literally—but this is not the Catholic Church's historic understanding of the eucharistic texts. We believe that the elements *are*, rather only symbolically *represent*, Jesus' body and blood.

John: How do the words of the celebrating priest turn the communal elements—the bread and wine—into the body and blood of Jesus? I am not sure how this works. Or is it just a mystery?

Dwight: The Catholic Church teaches that it is Christ himself who empowers the sacraments, which he does through priests and others who perform the rite. In the celebration of the Eucharist, it is the risen Lord who transforms the bread and wine into his body and blood. The word *transubstantiation* is used to describe what we believe happens in the consecration of the bread and wine; the actual process of transformation, however, remains a mystery.

Another difference between the Protestant and Catholic celebrations of the Lord's Supper is that, for Catholics, Christ's sacrifice is re-presented or presented anew. (Some Protestants mistakenly think that Catholics believe that Christ is re-sacrificed in the celebration of the Eucharist. This is an incorrect understanding of the Catholic Eucharist.) The priest signifies Christ's sacrifice during the eucharistic prayer when he consecrates the elements. Though not widely practiced today, bells are rung to announce the consecration of the elements, the holiest moment in the Mass. (Bells were first used in the Middle Ages because, in large Gothic cathedrals, many could not hear the words of the celebrating priest and needed a signal to announce the moment of consecration.) The understanding of Christ's *sacrifice* in the celebration of Holy Eucharist is clearly more important in Catholicism than it is in non-sacramental Protestant denominations.

John: The sacrifice of Christ is very prominent in Catholicism. One example is the wafer offered to communicants, which is called the 'host,' from the Latin *hostia*, meaning 'victim.' Another is the cross, which in most Catholic churches depicts Christ hanging on the cross. In most Protestant churches, crosses are empty, signifying Christ's victory over death. Why is there so much emphasis in Catholicism on Christ's sacrifice?

Dwight: Paul said, "We preach Christ crucified" (1 Corinthians 1:23). So do Catholics. I remember from my evangelical days hearing powerful sermons on the suffering and death of Jesus. We sang hymns like *There is Power in the Blood* and *The Old Rugged Cross*, which rightly focused our attention on the cross of Christ. It would be wrong, however, to think that Catholics focus on the cross to the exclusion of the resurrection. When you look at the interior imagery in most Catholic churches you see a portrayal of the resurrection. Catholics are Easter people, and always have been.

Regarding Jesus' crucifixion, we believe that Christ's death on the cross was the sacrifice that won our salvation. We also believe that through the Mass, Christ's saving death and resurrection is made available to each of us in and through the Eucharist.

Attendance at Sunday Mass—or Saturday vigil Mass, following the Jewish custom that 'after sundown' means the next calendar day—is obligatory for Catholics, and missing Mass without a legitimate excuse is a mortal sin. According to a 2004 Gallup poll, the number of Catholics who attend Sunday Mass in the United States has declined to 45 percent (from a high of 74 percent in 1955). This percentage may seem low, but the percent of Catholics who attend Sunday Mass in the United States is much higher than it is for Catholics worldwide. In Europe, where secularism is very entrenched, the percentage of Catholics who attend Sunday Mass is well less than half of what it is in the United States.

John: According to the *Catechism of the Catholic Church*, Catholics "are obliged to participate in the Eucharist on days of obligation [Sunday and feast days], unless excused for serious reason ... Those who deliberately fail in this obligation commit a grave [meaning mortal] sin" (Article 2181). Are Catholics who miss Mass, which today is some 60 percent of Catholics worldwide, in jeopardy of losing their salvation if they are not excused from this obligation?

Dwight: Catholics are obliged to attend Mass because of the fourth commandment: "Keep holy the Sabbath day." But there is more to it than just obeying a law. Once we understand the centrality of the Mass—the Eucharist—it is a sin to skip Mass without a good reason. Why? Because when we skip Mass we separate ourselves from the body of Christ.

When the Catholic Church says that missing Mass is a mortal sin, she is not being legalistic. Instead, she is teaching that to continue in an attitude that disregards God's greatest gift to us—the gift of his Son—is to step onto a path that leads to death. Protestants sometimes ask Catholics, "Have you accepted Jesus into your life?" The Catholic answer is, "Yes, every time I go to Mass." To miss Mass intentionally is to reject Christ's sacrificial death for our sins, and all Christians would agree that to reject Christ can only lead to death.

John: In Catholicism, there are masses for the sick, the Requiem Mass (from a Latin word meaning 'rest,' now called the Mass of Christian Burial), the Nuptial (marriage) Mass, masses for those in purgatory, and masses for special occasions such as anniversaries. How do these masses relate to Jesus' sacrificial death and resurrection?

Dwight: The Mass is sometimes called the Great Prayer. In the Mass we pray for God's healing power to be applied to our individual and communal needs. We have evidence going back to the early centuries that Christians celebrated masses for their departed loved ones. The prayer of the Mass can also function as a special act of blessing. At weddings and anniversaries, the prayer of the Mass is said with a special intention, focusing God's blessing on the people who are celebrating an occasion of joy. At funerals, prayers are offered for the bereaved family and for the person who has died, asking that God's healing and forgiveness won by Christ on Calvary be applied to them.

THE TRIDENTINE SACRAMENTS
Confirmation, Reconciliation, Matrimony, Holy Orders and Anointing the Sick

At the Council of Trent (1545-1563), the Catholic Church formally adopted a sevenfold sacramental system. The sacraments in addition to baptism and Holy Communion or Eucharist are confirmation, the confirming of one's faith and the confirmand's initiation into the Church; reconciliation, the confession of, penance for and absolution of post-baptismal sins; matrimony, the covenanting of two people to each other in the eyes of God; holy orders, the consecration of those called to priestly vocations; and anointing the sick, the sacrament of healing, which is given to those who are ill or near death's door. The five additional sacraments are sometimes called the *Tridentine* sacraments, because they were made official Catholic doctrine at the Council of Trent.

Confirmation: Affirmation and Sealing the Holy Spirit. Baptism must be followed by a profession of faith; the sacrament of confirmation is where this happens. I remember my confirmation, when I was fifteen years old, at Saint Stephen's Episcopal Church in Minneapolis. It was a 'rite of passage' in my Christian life. The sacrament of confirmation is called the *service* of confirmation in most Protestant churches; it confirms the vows made by the confirmand's parents and godparents or sponsors at their baptism. Catholic confirmations of those raised in the faith usually take place when the confirmand is twelve years old.

The purpose of confirmation is to give confirmands an opportunity to study the church's teachings to strengthen their faith (the word confirmation comes from the Latin *confirmo*, meaning 'to strengthen') and to prepare them to confess their faith. In Catholicism, a bishop lays hands on and anoints the confirmand with the sign of the cross on his or her forehead, which signifies the transmission of the blessing of the sacrament and the sealing of the Holy Spirit. The biblical basis for conferring the Holy Spirit by the laying on of hands comes from Acts 8:14-17: "Peter and John placed their hands on [baptized believers in Samaria] and they received the Holy Spirit."

Protestants also confirm those who have been baptized earlier, but not as a sacrament because they find no scriptural attestation that Jesus commanded his followers to confirm those who had been baptized. In Protestantism, confirmation admits those confirmed into full membership in the church. According to Catholic journalist David Gibson, in his book *The Coming Catholic Church*, upwards of 40 percent of young Catholics in the West are not confirmed, indicating a decline in the observance of this sacrament in Europe and North America. In the rest of the Catholic world, the percentage of young people being confirmed is said to be much higher.

John: In most Protestant churches, when a person is baptized, he or she receives the Holy Spirit in all his fullness. Catholicism seems to believe in a two-step process: the receipt of the Spirit at baptism, which is sealed when the confirmand is anointed at his or her confirmation. Is it true that the gift of the Holy Spirit is only provisionally received at baptism? Furthermore, if the one being confirmed receives the fullness of the Spirit when the bishop lays his hands on the confirmand's head, what happens if a bishop is not present? Is a priest able to anoint the confirmand with the fullness of the Holy Spirit?

Dwight: While the Holy Spirit is present at baptism, confirmation is the sacrament that seals and strengthens the Spirit's presence in the confirmand. And yes, a priest may confirm and anoint a confirmand if a bishop delegates this duty to him.

Reconciliation: Confession, Penance and Absolution. When I was in high school, my Catholic friends talked about having to go to confession and doing penance. (Confession is the acknowledgment of one's sins; penance is the payment or punishment for such sins.) Since Vatican II, the sacrament of confession or penance has been called the sacrament of reconciliation, meaning the forgiveness of and penance for sins so that one may be 'reconciled' with God. For the sacrament to be valid, there must be contrition (genuine sorrow); penitents must acknowledge and confess their sins orally to a priest; and they must agree to do acts of penance, such as praying the rosary, fasting and doing works of service. If the penitent does these three things, the priest absolves the penitent of his or her sins. His power to do so comes from his capacity as an ordained 'priest' in the church of Jesus Christ.

Jesus forgave sins, as indicated in the story of the paralytic who was lowered through the roof of a house in Capernaum (Matthew 9:1-8). Catholics believe that Jesus passed his authority to forgive sins on to his disciples when he said, "If you forgive the sins of any, they are forgiven" (John 20:23). The biblical text that Catholics use to support the sacrament of reconciliation is James 5:16, which talks about confessing sins "to one another"—in Catholicism, to a priest. Protestants believe in each person's direct access to God through Christ: "For there is one God [and] there is *one mediator* between

God and humankind, Jesus Christ" (1 Timothy 2:5). When Catholics go to a priest for confession, they believe they are going to Christ himself, because it is Christ, in and through the priest, who forgives their sins. One benefit in the Catholic sacrament of reconciliation is the cleansing effect that comes from oral confession.

John: I understand that if a Catholic is alone at the moment of death, on a battlefield, for instance, he or she can make a saving confession to Christ, though I imagine this relates only to venial sins. If this is so, why can't Catholics make private confessions at others times as well?

Dwight: Catholics can privately confess their sins to Christ at any time; we don't need to be alone on a battlefield to do this. However, men and women are not always the best critics of their own spiritual condition. A priest is often able to see us better than we can see ourselves; furthermore, he is empowered to administer the grace of Christ's forgiveness through the sacrament of reconciliation.

John: I have never understood Catholicism's division of sins into *venial* (forgivable or pardonable) and *mortal* (grave or deadly). Why is it necessary to have two classes of sins—junior sins and senior sins? In the Lord's Prayer we pray, "Forgive us our trespasses." There is no distinction in the prayer between different kinds of sins: any and all 'trespasses' are *sins*.

Dwight: The distinction between venial and mortal sins is found in 1 John 5:16-17. Venial sins are those sins which occur through the everyday rough and tumble of life. If we are living a life of faith, venial sins are purged through God's grace and living lives of prayer and worship and doing acts of mercy. If the purification process is not completed in this life, then it continues in purgatory. Mortal sins are different and more serious; in fact, they are deadly. Mortal sins are those sins that we deliberately plan and carry through. The severity is much worse because we enjoy the sin and don't intend to give it up. Such sins, if not confessed and forgiven, *may* deny one the eternal salvation of his or her soul. This is not because of any judgmental legalism, but because these sins lead the sinner away from God. Dealing with venial sins is like weeding a flower bed: the weeds just grow. In the Christian life, by God's grace, we pull them out. If we don't finish weeding the bed here, the work continues after death. Mortal sin is just the opposite: it is pulling out the flowers and planting weeds instead.

Matrimony: "And the Two Shall Become One Flesh." When I grew up, it was rare to hear of a Catholic marrying a non-Catholic; such marriages were often referred to as 'mixed marriages.' Not today. The sacrament of matrimony or marriage is the covenanting of two people together in the eyes of God: "and the two shall become one flesh" (Genesis 2:24). Jesus affirms the Genesis verse in Matthew 19:5-6 and Mark 10:7-8. In contrast with the other sacraments, which involve the conferring of sacramental grace by bishops and priests, the sacrament of matrimony is conferred by the two people being married, with vows to one another. The role of the officiating priest is to preside over the ceremony and give his *nuptial* (from a Latin word meaning 'to marry') blessing to the marriage.

Catholicism considers marriage to be indissoluble—'once married, always married'—even for spouses trapped in abusive relationships. Ambrose, the fourth-century bishop of Milan, was the first to teach that no marriage could be dissolved, even in the case of adultery, which seems contrary to Jesus' teaching in Matthew 5:32 and 19:9, where divorce was allowed "for unchastity." Augustine, a protégé of Ambrose, taught that matrimony is a sacrament.

If a Catholic man or woman wishes to divorce (obtain a legal dissolution of his or her marriage) and remarry, there must be an annulment, a formal church declaration that the marriage was invalid from the beginning due to some sacramental or other deficiency. Prior to 1983, annulments had to be approved in Rome.

Today, according to Catholic historian Garry Wills, annulments are both widespread and easily obtained: there are more than 60,000 annulments each year in the United States, and 90 percent of those who apply for an annulment receive one. One explanation may be that marriages that are entered into lightly, as often happens today, can be sacramentally deficient or invalid. Notwithstanding the large number of annulments, the Catholic Church should be applauded for taking marriage vows seriously—more seriously, I suspect, than do most Protestant churches.

John: I don't understand how matrimony can be a sacrament. Sacraments impart grace. In the 'sacrament' of matrimony, the church is not really involved, other than to bless the marriage. How does God's 'grace' get conferred in the sacrament of matrimony?

Dwight: In marriage, the two people who marry confer God's grace on each other through their mutual covenant before witnesses in the church, and through their promise to be faithful to one another. This is an example of the Catholic belief in the 'priesthood of all believers.' In the Eucharist, an ordained priest administers the sacrament; in the sacrament of matrimony, ordinary men and women administer the sacrament to each other.

John: If a Catholic marriage is annulled or invalidated, were the two 'spouses' living in sin (the sin of fornication) during the years they lived together? And are children who were born during an 'invalid' marriage considered, in the eyes of the Catholic Church, to be illegitimate?

Dwight: The validity of a marriage is determined by church tribunals; sacraments are valid until proven invalid. A couple who *thought* they were married sacramentally in the eyes of the church would not be living in sin; they would be culpable only if they *knew* their marriage was sacramentally invalid. To answer your second question, the Catholic Church does not consider children born of a sacramentally invalid marriage to be illegitimate.

John: The sin of adultery is a mortal sin. Are Catholics who remarry without having their former marriages annulled in danger of losing their salvation?

Dwight: I am no expert on Catholic canon law. As I understand it, if a Catholic has been validly married, and gets a civil divorce but does not have his or her previous marriage annulled, and marries another person, you are correct in saying that he or she is living in a state of mortal sin. If this happens, the man's or woman's soul is in danger, though the danger is directly proportionate to the divorced man's or woman's understanding of the church's teaching on divorce and remarriage, as explained by a priest, and the person's own conscience. However, the situation is usually not as complicated as this. If a priest knows that a person is living in such a state, he is obliged to point this out and either find a way to help such persons validate their relationship or, if need be, refuse them Holy Eucharist should they present themselves in church. In practice, of course, this is very difficult.

Marriage discipline is a hornet's nest for every Christian church, because the ideal of a lifelong, loving marriage and the reality of humankind's fallen condition are so far apart. As you've hinted, the whole process is fraught with difficulties, inconsistencies and incredible complexities. Nevertheless, I am hugely impressed by the Catholic Church's willingness to wrestle with this issue—and quite frankly, the alternatives don't seem much better. Beneath it all is the Catholic Church's dedication to the ideal of purity within the body of Christ.

Holy Orders: The Consecration of Those Called to Ministry. As a young boy I always admired the dedication and singleness of priests, and enjoyed movies like *Boy's Town*, with Spencer Tracy playing Father Flannigan, and *Going My Way*, with Bing Crosby and Barry Fitzgerald. Catholic men become priests through the sacrament of holy orders, which Protestants call ordination, though they don't consider ordination to be a sacrament. (Luther said that ordination was not a sacrament because all believers are called to be priests, based on his reading of 1 Peter 2:9.) During the sacrament of holy orders, priests make vows or promises to God to live lives of poverty, chastity and obedience.

In Protestantism, there is less of a formal divide between the clergy and the laity than there is in Catholicism, though this is slowly beginning to change: since Vatican II, the liturgy is in the vernacular and priests face the congregation rather than the altar when consecrating the bread and wine in the celebration of Holy Eucharist. Also, in most branches of Protestantism since the second half of the twentieth century, women have been ordained into the clergy. And in those denominations that have bishops—Episcopal, Lutheran (though not Missouri Synod Lutheran) and Methodist—women have also become bishops. Today there are an estimated 50,000 female Protestant pastors in the United States. In contrast, as everyone knows, the Catholic clergy is exclusively male.

Protestantism has found women to be gifted preachers and youth leaders and, pastorally, often more effective than men in dealing with illness, death, divorce and family matters. The Catholic Church has drawn on feminine gifts through its many orders of nuns, which have been 'ministering' far longer than the relatively recent ordination of Protestant women. Nevertheless, according to a recent Lilly Foundation survey, the overwhelming majority of American Catholics favor the ordination of women. Having a male-only clergy seems, to many, to be very medieval, resulting in pleas by American Catholics to end the practice, which the Vatican refuses to hear or even consider. The papacy is often blamed for this conservatism, but the real reason may be that Catholics in Asia, Africa and Latin America—who are far more numerous than those in America (American Catholics represent only 6 percent of Catholics worldwide)—are opposed to women priests.

John: I find it puzzling that the Vatican continues to insist—with a declining core of priests to serve a church that is forecast by the *World Christian Encyclopedia* to grow by 500 million parishioners between now and the year 2050—that its clergy be male-only. Are the Catholic Church's arguments for a male-only priesthood relevant today? Isn't it more important to have women priests to celebrate the sacraments than to deny them to believers in parishes where there are no priests?

Dwight: American Catholics are in the forefront of those who wish the Catholic Church would begin ordaining women into the priesthood. Philip Jenkins points out in *The Next Christendom*, however, that the vast majority of Catholics in the world do not consider women's ordination an important issue.

The Catholic Church does acknowledge that there are many gifts that women bring to ministry, and it is working hard to find more ways for these gifts to be exercised within the church. The priesthood, however, was instituted by Christ himself, and he chose men to be his apostles, even though he had many women followers. Further, the priest represents Christ in the celebration of the Eucharist, which means that those who *re-present* Christ to their congregations must be males. Social and cultural reasons may abound for changing something in Catholicism, but that doesn't mean it will be changed. Historical precedent carries great weight in the Catholic Church.

John: You give the traditional argument for a male-only priesthood, but advocates for women priests say that the argument that "this is the way it has always been" is not very compelling in this day and age. They say that a male-only priesthood developed out of a patriarchal culture, which no longer exists. As for the argument that only males can properly represent Christ, advocates for women in the priesthood say that we are all called to be priests, not just men; and this being so, women should be allowed to exercise the office of priesthood.

Another issue where Catholics and Protestants are not on the same page is celibacy, which Catholics claim comes from a special *charism* (gift) that allows men and women called by God to live celibate lives. Celibacy was voluntary in the early church; it did not become canon law until the Second Lateran Council in 1139. For the first thousand or so years there was no requirement that priests be celibate. Jesus praised marriage and nowhere made celibacy a condition of discipleship. Peter, whom Catholics look back on as the first pope, was married (Mark 1:30-31; 1 Corinthians 9:5); and he and his wife apparently had a daughter, whose name comes down to us as Petronilla. And given the norm for Jewish males in the first century, there is good reason to believe that other of Jesus' disciples may have been married as well. Furthermore, the apostle Paul claimed the right to marry (1 Corinthians 9:5), which he did not exercise; and he wrote to Timothy to select as overseers of his churches men who had been "married only once" (1 Timothy 3:2).

It has long been claimed that unmarried priests have more time to fulfill their priestly duties. It is doubtful that this is true today, with the decline in the priest-to-parishioner ratio. In the United States, the ratio was 1 to 1,100 in 1970; 1 to 2,100 in 1990; and is believed to be 1 to 3,100 in the year 2005. The Vatican continues to deny there is a clergy problem, notwithstanding the fact that fewer young men are *entering* the priesthood and more (especially young) priests are *leaving* the priesthood. However, this may be more of a western problem than a world problem: it is said that the number of Catholic priests in the developing world is actually growing.

Celibacy is not a natural state for men or women, nor is it biblical: God told Adam, "It is not good for man to be alone" (Genesis 2:18). On the other hand, Jesus was celibate, and he applauds celibacy "for the sake of the kingdom" (Matthew 19:12). And the apostle Paul was celibate, and he recommended celibacy as a way to devote oneself totally to the Lord's service (1 Corinthians 7:21-38). Nevertheless, priestly celibacy is probably a big reason for the low number of males entering the priesthood, at least in the West. In some countries the number of men entering seminaries on their way to priesthood is down by 50 percent over the past twenty-five years, and the primary reason for this is celibacy. It is estimated that soon half of all Catholic churches in the world will not have priests, depriving Catholics in such churches the opportunity to celebrate Holy Eucharist, which for Catholics is the most important sacrament. According to a recent Gallup poll, 75 percent of American Catholics said they opposed priestly celibacy. But this isn't just a Catholic issue or problem; the number of Protestant ministers is falling as well, and this has nothing to do with celibacy because Protestant clergy can marry.

John: Do you think that celibacy should be exclusive or optional, as it is in Eastern Rite Catholic Churches, which has some 5,000 married priests?

Dwight: In harmony with Jesus and Paul, both of whom were celibate, the Catholic Church values and commends this discipline, while not requiring it for all. Because it is not a command of the Lord, celibacy, unlike the gender of priests, is merely a discipline of the church. Theoretically it could change tomorrow. I am among those who wish the Catholic Church would adopt the Eastern Orthodox discipline that values both celibacy and marriage among its clergy. However, I am under no illusion that allowing priests to marry will solve any of the church's problems. My experience as a Protestant leads me to suspect that having married clergy is likely to create, instead, a whole new set of problems for the Catholic Church.

Anointing the Sick: Prayers of Healing and Preparation for Death. When I grew up, what is now called anointing the sick was called *extreme* (from *in extremis*, meaning near death) *unction* (meaning anointing); it was also called the last rites. From the earliest days, Catholic clergy anointed the sick. Peter Lombard, the bishop of Paris, was the first to include extreme unction as a sacrament. It was numbered among the seven sacraments from the thirteenth century on, and made official at the Council of Trent in the sixteenth century. The name extreme unction was changed to anointing the sick in 1972, and broadened to include those who were seriously ill, including those about to undergo serious operations (the sacrament is also called the sacrament of healing). The scriptural bases for the sacrament are Jesus' charge to his disciples to "Heal the sick" (Mark 6:13 and Matthew 10:8) and James' advice that if any are sick, "[The] elders of the church should pray over them, anointing them with oil in the name of the Lord" (James 5:13-16). The oil used in anointing those who are infirm, called 'oil of the sick,' is specially blessed for this purpose by a bishop.

John: I understand that anointing those who are sick or elderly or are in danger of dying washes away all post-baptismal sins in case they die. This seems at odds with the sacrament of reconciliation, where a penitent must first acknowledge and confess his or her sins. Is anointing the sick an end-run around the confessional aspect of reconciliation? And because 'anointing' washes away one's sins, are those who have been anointed saved from purgatory?

Dwight: The sacrament of healing is linked with the forgiveness of sin and includes both confession and absolution, wherever possible. If a person is too ill to make a confession, the priest looks for some small sign of repentance. If that is impossible, then the healing and forgiving power of the sacrament takes effect by God's mercy. Such a person would be forgiven his or her sins, but that would not exempt them from purgatory, which has to do with purging the debt of punishment that sin incurs.

Chapters 4, 5, and 6 dealt with matters about which Protestants and Catholics disagree. The next and final chapter has to do with matters that are, for the most part, specific or unique to Catholicism. They include sacramentals such as the rosary, holy water, candles and genuflection; books in the Catholic Old Testament that do not appear in Protestant versions of the Bible; the need to purge one's soul of venial sins before going to heaven; and the veneration of saints.

CHAPTER SEVEN

Unique Catholic Beliefs and Practices

Standard Equipment or Optional Extras?

There are several Catholic beliefs and practices that are not found in Protestantism. Four of these are examined below: sacramentals such as the rosary, holy water, candles, incense and genuflection; several so-called 'deuterocanonical' books that are not in the Protestant Old Testament canon; the belief that those who die with unforgiven venial sins go to purgatory to have their souls purified before proceeding on to heaven; and the beatification, canonization and veneration of saints.

CATHOLIC SACRAMENTALS
The Rosary, Water, Genuflection and More

In addition to the seven sacraments in Chapter 6, Catholics also have *sacramentals*, physical objects or aspects of worship that are common to many religions. Sacramentals do not *convey* grace; rather, they prepare or dispose one to *receive* grace. Sacramentals are qualitatively different than sacraments: sacraments have their origin in Christ; sacramentals have their origin in the Church.

The following are some popular sacramentals, and this is mainly for Protestants because most Protestants know very little about Catholic sacramentals. For Catholics, holy water, candles, incense, votive (vowed) candles, the rosary, the sign of the cross, bells and the rest are part and parcel of Catholic life, and something I never quite got my mind around when I went to church with Catholic friends.

The most popular sacramental is the *rosary*, from the word *rosarium*, meaning rose garden (the rose is one of the flowers used to symbolize Mary). Praying or saying the rosary is a devotional practice consisting of the recitation of a series of prayers that go back to Saint Dominic in the thirteenth century. (According to legend, the words of the rosary were revealed by Mary to Dominic.) The rosary chain has a series of prayer beads, divided into five 'decades' (tens) associated with different events in Jesus' life. The center of the prayer is as follows: "Hail Mary, full of grace, the Lord is with thee. Blessed art thou among women, and blessed is the fruit of thy womb, Jesus. Holy Mary, Mother of God, pray for us sinners now and at the hour of our death." The first two sentences of the prayer come from Luke 1:28 and 1:42; scriptural verses underlie the rest of the prayer as well. The rosary helps Catholics meditate daily on the Gospels and draw closer to Jesus. To pray the full rosary, one goes around the chain three times, making 150 prayers. This was a way for lay people in the Middle Ages to connect with the Bible-based worship of monks, who recited all 150 Psalms each week in their worship.

The most widely-used sacramental is *holy water*, which is usually found in a font or stoup inside the front door of Catholic churches. Catholics dip two fingers of their right hand into the water and make the sign of the cross when they enter the church, which symbolically cleanses them. (Ritual cleansing upon entering a house of worship is practiced in many religions.) It connects the believer back to ritual cleansings that Jesus and his disciples would have done as faithful Jews, and reminds them of their water baptism into the body of Christ.

Burning *incense*, or more specifically the rising of incense smoke, symbolizes the rising of prayers to God, similar to rabbis in Jerusalem

Unique Catholic Beliefs and Practices

who burn petitions to God placed between the stones in the Western or Wailing Wall on the Day of Atonement, with the smoke carrying the petitions heavenward. Incense is used by Catholic churches on solemn occasions, and by Eastern Orthodox churches, and also some Anglican/Episcopal churches. The use of incense goes back to the story of Zechariah entering the temple to burn incense (Luke 1:8-9), where he is told by the angel Gabriel that he and his wife Elizabeth are to have a son.

Some Catholics wear necklaces with cross-adorned coin-like medals. Others wear scapulars, which are small squares of cloth that represent the religious habit of a monk or nun. When these items are blessed, they are considered holy objects and serve as constant reminders of a Catholic's commitment to a life of prayer and holiness. The blessing of physical objects is rooted in Jewish tradition, where vestments and articles of worship were blessed by priests. In the New Testament, certain physical objects contained spiritual power, as in the story in Acts where handkerchiefs and aprons that touched Paul "were brought to the sick [and] their diseases left them, and the evil spirits came out of them" (Acts 19:11-12).

When entering church, many Catholics bend down on their right knee before taking their seat to acknowledge the presence of Christ. This is called *genuflection*, from two Latin words meaning 'to bend the knee.' Catholics also genuflect when passing in front of the altar on which resides the Blessed Sacrament, the consecrated body of Christ that remains after the celebration of the Eucharist. When Catholics bow their knee in the presence of God, they are reminded that "Every knee should bend ... and every tongue should confess that Jesus Christ is Lord" (Philippians 2:10-11).

Another sacramental is the stations of the cross—fourteen 'stations' depicting fourteen scenes from the passion of Christ. The stations grew out of a practice that dates back to antiquity, when pilgrims traveled to Jerusalem to visit sites associated with Christ's suffering and death. When this became impossible due to the

Muslim control of Jerusalem, or difficult or impractical to travel long distances to the Holy Land, scenes depicting Jesus' passion were carved into church walls and used for devotions during Lent and Holy Week.

John: How important are the sacramentals to the average Catholic? Which are the most important to you, and for what reason?

Dwight: Sacramentals are optional extras; they are not part of Catholic dogma. Their purpose is to help the faithful on their spiritual journey. In addition to the sacramentals above, there are three that you didn't mention: going on pilgrimages to holy places like Rome, Jerusalem and famous Catholic shrines; lighting candles before images of saints; and offering flowers and works of art to decorate churches and honor God and his saints.

The physical side of worship is similar in ways to Jewish worship—the tabernacle and temple, the laver and incense bowls, carvings and rich embroidery, and priest's vestments. All of this sounds far closer to Catholic worship than to that of Protestantism. But again, sacramentals are not *essentials*; it is more a case of 'to each his own.' There are lots of Catholics who don't connect physical aspects like sacramentals to their worship, just like most Protestants. For me, personally, sacramentals make my worship real, concrete and physical. The sacramentals that mean most to me are saying the rosary, lighting candles and embarking on pilgrimages.

CANONICITY
The Catholic Old Testament

Protestants and Catholics (and Eastern Orthodox) have the same twenty-seven books in their New Testaments. Their Old Testaments, however, are different: Catholics have forty-six books and Protestants thirty-nine books. The seven additional books in the Catholic Old Testament come from the *Septuagint*, which both Catholic and Orthodox churches consider divinely inspired. The word 'Septuagint' comes from the Greek *septuaginta*, meaning 'seventy,' the nearest round number for the seventy-two rabbis (six from each of the twelve tribes) who, according to legend, went to Alexandria, Egypt, around the year 250 BC and translated the Hebrew scriptures into Greek, the *lingua franca* (common language) of the ancient world, so they could be read by Greek-speaking Jews in Egypt.

There are fifteen books in the *Septuagint* which do not appear in the Hebrew canon. Most Jews living in Alexandria considered these books part of the Bible, and Jewish Christians living in Alexandria did so as well. Augustine considered them canonical, and early church fathers in both the East and West quoted them as scripture without distinction.

When the church moved its center westward and became Latin-speaking, there was need for a Latin translation of the scriptures so that people could read the Bible in their own language. In the year 382, Pope Damasus asked Jerome, the greatest scholar and linguist of his day, to translate the Old and New Testaments into Latin. Jerome completed his translation in 405, which came to be called the *Vulgate*, from a Latin word meaning 'common' or 'ordinary' (language). Jerome followed ancient tradition and included twelve of the Septuagintal books in his translation, with a word of caution from Jewish scholars with whom he worked that the books, while edifying, were not to be considered as having the same degree of canonicity as the books in the Hebrew canon. Over time these *deuterocanonical* ('second canon') books were recognized by the Catholic Church as having equal status with the books in the Hebrew Bible; at the Council of Trent they were declared to be fully canonical. The deuterocanonical books are also found in the Eastern Orthodox Old Testament, which is based on the Greek Septuagint—in fact, the Orthodox Old Testament has fifty books; the additional four books are 1 Esdras, 3 Maccabees, the Prayer of Manasseh and Psalm 151.

When Martin Luther and the Reformers translated the Bible into German, English and other languages, they put the deuterocanonical books in a separate section between the Old and New Testaments—between Malachi and Matthew—called the *Apocrypha*, from a Greek word denoting writings of questionable authorship or authenticity because they had not been received into the Jewish canon. Although these books are not in the Protestant Old Testament, they are important documents. Books such as 1 and 2 Maccabees provide a history of God's people during the period between the Old and New Testaments. Other books reflect changes that began to emerge in Jewish thinking, one being the belief in an afterlife, which is only briefly alluded to in the Hebrew scriptures.

Seven of the Septuagintal books were added to the Old Testament canon to make forty-six books. *Tobit* is the story of a pious, law-abiding Jew whose blindness is healed by the magic formulas of an angel, Raphael. *Judith* is the story of a beautiful widow who, like Esther, saves her people. *First and Second Maccabees* contain stories of the repressive regime of Antiochus Epiphanes (reign: 175-163 BC) and the revolt and cleansing of the temple in Jerusalem in the year 164 BC under the leadership of Judas Maccabeus, an event that Jews celebrate as *Hanukkah* ('dedication'), an eight-day festival that occurs around the same time of year as Christmas. *Baruch* is a book attributed to the secretary of Jeremiah, to which was added *The Letter of Jeremiah*, written to those about to be taken into captivity by the Babylonians. The *Wisdom of Solomon* has to do with the origin, nature and function of wisdom, and the fate of those who do good and those who do evil. *Ecclesiasticus* is a collection of sayings and advice similar to the book of Proverbs.

Five other Septuagintal books were added to existing books in the Catholic Old Testament. They are *The Letter of Jeremiah*, mentioned above, which was added to the book of *Baruch*; *Additions to Esther*, which was added to the book of Esther to give it a more 'religious' feel (the name of God is not mentioned in the canonical book of Esther); and three additions to the book of Daniel: *The Prayer of Azariah* and *The Song of the Three Friends*, the prayer of Daniel's three companions in the fiery furnace (Daniel 3:24-90); *Susanna*, the story of two wicked elders who desire the beautiful Susanna, who is rescued by Daniel (Daniel 13); and *Bel and the Dragon*, a tale set in the time of Daniel which contrasts the true worship of God with the false worship of the Babylonian gods (Daniel 14).

John: Why did the Council of Trent add the deuterocanonical books to the Hebrew (Old Testament) canon? Did they do this because they considered the Septuagint divinely inspired? Or was it a move against Luther? Or was there another reason?

Dwight: It is not correct to say the Council of Trent 'added' books to the Old Testament canon. These books were part of the Christian canon as far back as Jerome, and most canonical lists from that time forward included them. What Trent did was to confirm books that the ancient church had long considered canonical.

The Church's role is to define and defend the faith, but it usually does so only when the faith is being attacked. The canon is a good example. For eleven hundred years—from Jerome's *Vulgate* in 405 to the beginning of the Reformation in 1517—the Bible included several so-called deuterocanonical books. When the Reformers removed these books from the Bible, the Catholic Church stepped forward and defined the canon of scripture to include them.

PURGATORY
The Intermediate State

In Catholicism, purgatory is a temporary stopping place between earth and heaven to purge one's soul of unforgiven venial sins before entering into the divine presence of God. Peter Kreeft calls purgatory 'heaven's porch,' the place where one awaits final entry into heaven. For Catholics, though purgatory is a place of suffering for unforgiven sins, those in purgatory know that they are destined to enjoy eternal union with God.

The main scriptural support for purgatory comes from 2 Maccabees 12:42-46. This text mentions praying for the dead, though the context doesn't mention purgatory as such. Another verse that is sometimes appealed to is 1 Corinthians 3:15, which talks about being saved from the fire, presumably the flames of hell, though, again, purgatory is not mentioned. Prayers by family members to Mary and the saints are believed to be efficacious in shortening one's time in purgatory. After the soul has been purified, it proceeds on to heaven.

The Catholic doctrine of purgatory developed during the Middle Ages and became dogma at the Council of Trent. It is part of Catholicism's penitential system to explain how God's divine justice relates to those who die with unforgiven venial sins. The Reformers rejected purgatory as a denial of Jesus' all-sufficient salvific death: if Jesus died for our sins, there is no need for any post-death cleansing of the souls of believers. Furthermore, Jesus said to the so-called penitent thief on the cross, "*Today* you will be with me in paradise" (Luke 23:43), indicating that the souls of believers go straight to paradise (heaven?) rather than passing through purgatory.

It isn't clear how long souls spend in purgatory—or even if asking "How long?" is relevant, because there is no space and time in eternity. (One writer said, "Eternity is not a whole bunch of time; it is the absence of time.") Apparently it relates to the seriousness of one's unforgiven sins; but because venial sins are minor sins, it can't be very long. One way to move the souls of those in purgatory along to heaven is by offering prayers and special masses. Another way is to beseech Mary and the saints to intercede on behalf of those who have died. Because all believers are part of the 'communion of saints' on earth and in heaven, as the Apostles' Creed attests, it is natural to beseech those already in heaven to intercede with God on behalf of those who have recently died. Christians in all traditions offer intercessory prayers for those on earth; Catholics go further and pray for those who are or may be in purgatory.

John: I don't understand *why* purgatory is necessary, that is, why Jesus' once-for-all-time atoning death requires further purifying steps for baptized believers.

Dwight: Purgatory is the place where we make recompense for unforgiven sins we have committed. If you hit a baseball through my window, and then come and apologize, I will forgive you, but I will also expect you to pay for the window. Though we are saved by Christ's death on the cross, if we die with unforgiven venial sins, they must be purified. Purgatory is where this takes place; purgatory is where we pay for the broken window.

John: How long does the purgation process take? I suppose there is no way to know whether the souls of loved ones who have departed are with the Lord or are still in purgatory. Do you pray for the souls of loved ones to be released from purgatory? If so, how long after a person has died do you continue to pray for his or her soul?

Dwight: How long do souls spend in purgatory? In my opinion the medieval church was too literal-minded and legalistic about purgatory. They spoke of certain prayers and actions eliminating so many years from purgatory. It's impossible to be that specific about the afterlife. We lovingly pray for our loved ones whenever we remember them, and leave the question of whether they are in purgatory or in heaven to God's loving mercy.

John: Mortal sins can be forgiven by a priest, but if one dies with unforgiven mortal sins on his or her soul, he or she is denied heaven. Why can venial sins be forgiven on earth and purged in purgatory, but mortal sins can only be forgiven on earth? This seems inconsistent.

Dwight: If you die with unconfessed mortal sin in your life, that means you have been living in a sin that you knew was serious and did nothing about it; in fact, you probably didn't intend to do anything about it. You loved your sin more than you loved God—and that can only lead to eternal death. If you die with unforgiven venial sin in your life, on the other hand, your soul is not in a state of rebellion against God; you've merely fallen prey to the flaws and foibles of being human in an unredeemed world.

THE SAINTS
Beatification, Canonization and Veneration

Two other unique Catholic practices are the *beatification* and *canonization* of persons who have lived lives of extraordinary obedience and holiness. In the early church, 'saintly' persons such as holy bishops, martyrs and doctors of the church were venerated. There was no formal canonization process until the reign of Pope Gregory IX who, in 1234, declared that only papal canonizations were valid. The three-step process by which one becomes a saint begins with the declaration that a person is 'venerable.' The next step is beatification, which cannot begin until a person has been deceased for five years. (Mother Teresa, who died in 1997, was beatified in 2003.) The life and writings of candidates whose names are put forward for beatification are carefully examined and investigated. One miracle must be verified for beatification, and another for canonization; for martyrs, no miracles are required for beatification.

When the pope canonizes a person, he declares that the deceased person has entered heaven and may be venerated (though not worshipped) as a saint, and can be petitioned by those on earth to intercede for them and for loved ones who are in purgatory. (Catholics do not pray to saints to intercede for them per se; they pray for saints to intercede with God on their behalf.) When the then-Catholic Martin Luther was caught in the thunderstorm at Stotternheim, he prayed to Saint Anne to intercede for him, and honored her by becoming an Augustinian monk. Once a person is declared a saint, a feast day is assigned and shrines and statues may be built in his or her honor.

John: In your book on Mary, you said, "At the end, I would rather be blamed for believing too much than too little." I like this. What do you believe about saints? Which are your favorite saints?

Dwight: One of the greatest things about being a Catholic is knowing and appreciating the wonderful lives of the saints. They are our brothers and sisters in Christ. They have completed and finished the great task to which we all are called. Protestants don't always acknowledge this, but they have great heroes of the faith as well, one example being the courageous missionaries who took the good news into remote areas of the world, many suffering deprivation, torture and death. Holiness is present in all churches; the Catholic Church is simply more formal in its appreciation of how magnificently God's grace can transform ordinary people.

Apart from the Blessed Virgin Mary, my favorite saints are Saint Benedict of Nursia, Saint Thérèse of Lisieux and Saint Joseph. I appreciate their heroism in the Christian faith, and their dignity and passion in finding the love and grace of God within the ordinary things of life.

Some Final Thoughts

In 1994 Father Richard John Neuhaus, a Lutheran pastor who in the 1980s became a Catholic priest and is now editor-in-chief of *First Things*, a monthly magazine 'to advance a religiously informed public philosophy for the ordering of society,' and Charles Colson, a Southern Baptist and the founder and president of Prison Fellowship, along with George Weigel and Kent Hill, wrote a document entitled *Evangelicals and Catholics Together: The Christian Mission in the Third Millennium* (*ECT*). Although widely welcomed by both Catholics and evangelicals, the document caused something of a furor. Some evangelicals thought *ECT* had given away too much, especially regarding the Protestant belief in justification by faith. Some Catholics thought *ECT* had compromised Catholic beliefs in order to accommodate evangelicals. Some months after the release of *ECT*, Walter Horton, the director of Christians United for Reformation, and J. I. Packer, professor of theology at Regent College, issued a revision that highlighted the different understandings of justification by faith, with evangelicals insisting on justification by faith *alone*; it also took issue with transubstantiation and various Marian doctrines.

Attempts were made in the last third of the twentieth century to bridge differences between Roman Catholics and several Protestant denominations—Lutherans, Anglicans, Pentecostals, Disciples of Christ, Baptists and others. The two longest dialogue meetings have been with Lutherans and Anglicans. The Catholic-Lutheran dialogue began in 1965. Catholic writer George Weigel, in his book *The Truth of Catholicism*, said that the Catholic-Lutheran dialogue "reached a climax in 1999 when the Catholic Church and the Lutheran World Federation jointly affirmed that, despite continuing differences in theological understanding, they held in common the truths involved in the doctrine that we are justified by grace through faith in Christ. Yet the hard fact remains that Lutherans and Catholics were no closer to ecclesial union in 1999 than they were in 1965." Regarding Catholic-Anglican discussions, which began in 1969, Weigel said, "By the late 1980s it became painfully clear that the Anglican/Roman Catholic dialogue had not moved the two communities closer to ecclesial union. This in turn raised serious questions about the claim, common throughout the twentieth century, that the English Reformation had been essentially a political separation and that there were no grave doctrinal issues between Anglicans and Roman Catholics."

The purpose of this book is not to reconcile Catholic-Protestant differences, as if they are minor in nature and can be easily harmonized. Its purpose is to highlight those areas of common agreement between the two traditions, and to discuss areas of disagreement so that Catholics and Protestants will better understand the background and reasons for their differences. In addition, the first part of the book sets out the history of the division of the church into its three main branches or streams, Roman Catholic, Eastern Orthodox and Protestant, which one rarely finds in books that explore differences between Catholics and Protestants. Another unique feature is the dialogue between the two authors. Most books on Catholicism and Protestantism are written from one side or the other, including all but a couple of those in 'A Guide to Further Reading' which follows. A back-and-forth dialogue is the only way to present Catholic and Protestant differences in a living format.

John's Concluding Comments. There are many differences between Protestants and Catholics, as we have seen in Chapters 3, 4, 5, 6 and 7. Before summarizing the issues for me, I want to say how much I have enjoyed my interaction with Dwight, and how much I learned from him about Catholicism. I raised questions that I was sure Dwight could not answer to my satisfaction; he convinced me otherwise. Both I and our readers owe him a big thank you.

The primary issues I have with Catholicism are threefold. The first has to do with salvation: are we justified by faith *alone* or by faith plus observing the sacraments and doing good works? This is the basic theological difference between Catholics and Protestants, and has been since Luther nailed his theses on the Castle Church door in Wittenberg five hundred years ago. I don't see any way to resolve this issue. Protestants believe that we are saved by faith alone, which expresses itself in believing, trusting and following Jesus and living under his lordship. Catholics believe that faith must be accompanied by regular observance of the sacraments, especially Holy Eucharist, through which God's grace grows in the believer, and doing works of love and charity, which are signs that authenticate one's faith.

The second issue has to do with the top-down authority, power and infallibility of the papacy and the role of the Magisterium, which, if I have this right, sets forth what Catholics must believe, which I find very confining. The reason the Reformers translated the Bible into the vernacular was to enable Christians to read the Bible in their own language so they could apply its teachings to their lives. One consequence of this has been Protestantism's wide-ranging denominationalism. Some see this as a negative; others see it as allowing Christians to worship in communities of like-minded believers, which gives enormous energy and life to such churches.

The third issue is of less importance than the first two; it has to do with the Catholic Church's male-only, celibate-only priesthood. Protestantism has married clergy and women clergy, and the laity is actively involved in matters of leadership, liturgy and teaching. Although the Catholic Church is finding new ways to involve the laity, its insistence on an unmarried male clergy seems like an outmoded way of shepherding a church that is expected to grow by 50 percent over the next fifty years. I don't see much chance of this changing, unless Pope Benedict XVI or some subsequent pope does something revolutionary, like Pope John XXIII did when he called Vatican II.

Most of the other matters are secondary issues. Apostolic succession has little to do with day-to-day issues of faith and life, and the Vatican has taken a 'go slow' attitude on *ex cathedra* papal pronouncements. The three Marian issues in Chapter 5 are, in my opinion, patently unscriptural, though recognizably important to Catholics. I view the sacraments as signs and symbols of grace, rather than as channels of grace. I don't believe in transubstantiation, but I do celebrate and observe Holy Communion as a special sacrament. The Tridentine sacraments—confirmation, reconciliation, matrimony, ordination and anointing the sick—may be helpful to Catholics in the practice of their faith, but I am not convinced that they convey, *ex opera operato*, sanctifying grace. Finally, I believe that the souls of believers who have died, like my son Jay, are with the Lord, not suffering in purgatory.

Dwight's Concluding Comments. The only issue I really have has to do with the different mindsets and perspectives to which Catholics and Protestants appeal when discussing issues that divide us one from another, differences that surfaced several times between John and me in our conversation with one another.

I love my Protestant friends and I'll always be grateful for the wonderful Christian upbringing I had within evangelicalism. I think it is easier for Protestants to have 'issues' with Catholicism because Protestantism, by its very history and nature, is a reaction against Catholicism. The Protestant mindset tends to be overly rationalistic and skeptical; somehow, it seems like Protestants—at least, my Protestant friends—are always 'protesting.'

In my experience, the Catholic mindset is far more accepting, open and inclusive. One of the things I love to do in discussions with non-Catholics is to show that everything they affirm, we also affirm. We usually differ only when they deny things. This has been the case in the present discussion. John quoted me as saying that I would rather be blamed for believing too much than too little. That's right! In all the key disagreements with non-Catholics, I want to say, "Why do you have to come at everything with such a negative attitude?" Take the issues of *sola fide* and papal authority. Catholics would agree with John's affirmations; we just don't go along with the denials. We agree that faith is vital, but we also believe that works are vital. We believe in top-down papal authority, but we also believe in bottoms-up grass-roots movements. Protestants, as I have said several times, see things as 'either-or'; Catholics see things as 'both-and.'

My main issue with Protestants, I guess, is that they tend to nurture a skeptical, doubting attitude. I want to ask, "What if your denial of Catholic beliefs results in your denying something greater and more magnificent than you could ever imagine? Is it really a good thing to believe less rather than more?" Most Protestants say they celebrate Holy Communion, but that the bread and wine are only symbols. Catholics believe the bread and wine are symbols too, but we go much further. We say that, by God's miraculous grace, the symbols affect what they signify. What harm is there in believing this, especially when it fits perfectly with scripture? When I say this, my Protestant friends are suspicious, sort of like the businessman who was so afraid to be taken in that he missed the biggest deal of his life.

Okay, I'm being a bit sharp to make my point, and I don't want to end on a negative note. I continue to be grateful for the great riches of my evangelical Protestant upbringing. I love the Catholic Church, but I'm not uncritical of her. I wish she could learn some of the great strengths of Protestantism and become even stronger in her witness to the faith. I believe the twenty-first century will see a greater convergence of our two traditions, and I hope this book might play a part in bringing this about.

A Guide to Further Reading

The following are suggested readings for Catholics and Protestants who want to know more about their own and each other's faith, beliefs and practices. Much of the information in *Why Do You Believe That?* comes from these books. The quotes come from the back covers of the books.

Ankerberg, John, and Weldon, John. *Protestants & Catholics: Do they Now Agree?* Eugene, OR: Harvest House Publishers, 1995. This book explores doctrinal differences and asks the question, "Has either side changed its mind?" In the words of John MacArthur, Grace Community Church, "[The authors] have done a superb job of explaining how Catholicism and evangelicalism differ with regard to the gospel. Presenting both sides even-handedly, they call readers to judge the issues biblically."

Armstrong, John. *Roman Catholicism: Evangelical Protestants Analyze What Divides and Unites Us*. Chicago: Moody Press, 1994. Thirteen essays on divisions between Roman Catholics and Evangelicals. According to Regent College professor of theology J. I. Packer, "This book is a 'must read' for all who want to come to grips with Roman Catholicism as it really is."

Bell, James S., and Sumner, Tracy Macon. *The Complete Idiot's Guide to the Reformation and Protestantism*. Indianapolis, IN: Alpha

Books, 2002. A helpful guide to the history, causes and forces that led to the Reformation. Jerry Root, Wheaton College professor of Christian education, believes, "The Western world will never be quite the same because of the Reformation, and thinking people would be wise to understand its influence. [This book] opens a door to an important part of the past and may equally open some doors to understanding the future."

Bettenson, Henry. *The Early Christian Fathers.* Oxford: Oxford University Press, 1956. This book, still in print, introduces and summarizes the writings of the first Christian thinkers. Invaluable reading for anyone who wants to know what the early Christians thought and believed.

Bokenkotter, Thomas. *A Concise History of the Catholic Church,* revised and expanded edition. New York: Image Books, 1990. Considered by many to be the best up-to-date, unified one-volume history of the events and thinking that shaped the course of Catholic thought and action over the past two millennia. The book's scope is enormous, but the author's clarity and conciseness make it easy-to-read.

_____. *Dynamic Catholicism: A Historical Catechism.* New York: Doubleday, 1992. In the words of *Publishers Weekly,* "The main doctrines and practices of the Catholic Church are presented here with clarity and a mastery of comprehensiveness, making [it] appropriate for the general reader."

Catechism of the Catholic Church, second edition. Washington, DC: Liberia Editrice Vaticana, 1994. The first new compendium of Catholic doctrine in more than four hundred years, which updates *The Catechism of the Council of Trent.* In the words of John Paul II, the new *Catechism* stands as "a sure norm for teaching the faith" and as "an authentic reference text."

Coffey, Tony. *Once a Catholic.* Eugene, OR: Harvest House, 1993. Author Tony Coffey grew up Catholic and now ministers in

Dublin, Ireland. Coffey's book asks and answers questions about scripture versus tradition, the papacy, the Mass, confession, the priesthood, Mary, purgatory and divorce.

Colson, Charles, and Neuhaus, Richard John, editors. *Your Word is Truth: A Project of Evangelicals and Catholics Together*. Grand Rapids, MI: William B. Eerdmans, 2002. This book comprises six essays that look at the historic rift between evangelical Protestants and Roman Catholics regarding Protestantism's *sola scriptura* and Catholicism's reliance on both scripture and tradition.

Currie, David B. *Born Fundamentalist, Born Again Catholic*. San Francisco: Ignatius Press, 1996. A book written by the son of a fundamentalist preacher and graduate of Trinity Evangelical Divinity School to explain to his fundamentalist and evangelical friends and family why he [Currie] became a Roman Catholic. In the opinion of another evangelical-turned-Catholic, Thomas Howard, "With great clarity and lucidity, [Currie] pursues every conceivable topic—biblical, ecclesiological, theological and historical—that arises in discussions [with evangelicals about the Catholic Church]."

Encyclopedia of Catholicism, Richard P. McBrien, editor. New York: HarperCollins, 1995. A comprehensive reference resource on the people, places, history, theology, art, sacraments and spirituality of the world's largest religious tradition. This book contains more than 4,200 entries by 280 experts on all aspects of Catholicism, with feature-length entries, a helpful pronunciation guide, 300 photographs and several maps and line drawings.

Erickson, Millard J. *Christian Theology*, second edition. Grand Rapids, MI: Baker Book House, 1998. According to J. I. Packer, Regent College professor of theology, "During the past decade, Millard Erickson's *Christian Theology* has established itself as the most widely used Protestant survey of Christian truth. Robustly evangelical, essentially conservative, thoroughly contemporary, its fair-minded breadth and meticulous analysis of options have won it consistent praise. Now updated, its usefulness as a text for students and as a resource for pastors and lay leaders will be even greater. It is altogether a masterly piece of work."

Finley, Mitch. *The Seeker's Guide to the Christian Story*. Chicago: Loyola Press, 1998. Catholic writer Mitch Finley tells the story of Christianity from a Catholic perspective through a series of essays on significant people and moments in church history: Jesus of Nazareth, the early church, the New Testament, Constantine, the church councils, the Crusades, the Inquisition, the Protestant Reformation, the Council of Trent, the Modernist crisis, and John XXIII and the Second Vatican Council. Easy to read and understand.

Gaillardetz, Richard R. *By What Authority? A Primer on Scripture, the Magisterium and the Sense of the Faithful*. Collegeville, MN: Liturgical Press, 2003. An introduction to the inspiration of the Bible, how scripture and tradition are related to one another, and the role of the pope and bishops in preserving the Christian faith. In the words of Most Rev. John R. Quinn, St. Patrick's Seminary, "This book is a lucid, balanced guide for the interested inquirer on such complex questions as the role of theologians, church authority and the various levels of church teaching."

Geisler, Norman L., and MacKenzie, Ralph E. *Roman Catholics and Evangelicals: Agreements and Differences*. Grand Rapids, MI: Baker Book House, 2002. A good reference work on points of agreement and disagreement between Catholics and Protestants. According to Gordon Conwell Theological Seminary scholar David Wells, "The virtue of this book is clarity. It cuts through the fog of confusion and uncertainty like a searchlight."

Gibson, David. *The Coming Catholic Church: How the Faithful Are Shaping a New American Catholicism*. San Francisco: Harper San Francisco, 2002. Gibson shows how a radical reformation is being unleashed that will likely change the American Catholic Church forever. A fast, interesting read. In the words of

University of Notre Dame professor of theology Lawrence Cunningham, "David Gibson analyzes the historical and theological roots of the sex scandal, profiles the priests and bishops responsible, speculates prudently on future forms of the church, and finally gives us some reason for hope."

Godfrey, Robert W. *Reformation Sketches: Insights into Luther, Calvin and the Confessions.* Phillipsburg, NJ: P & R Publishing, 2002. The author believes that, "The Reformers and preachers of the sixteenth century were the best educated, most godly and most faithful group of leaders the church has ever seen. We need to continue to learn from them."

Hahn, Scott and Kimberly. *Rome Sweet Home: Our Journey to Catholicism.* San Francisco: Ignatius Press, 1993. The journey of a Gordon-Conwell Seminary graduate and Presbyterian (PCA) pastor and his wife from evangelicalism to Roman Catholicism.

Hardon, John A., S.J. *Pocket Catholic Dictionary.* New York: Image Books, 1985. A comprehensive, one-volume reference work containing some 2,000 definitions and explanations of the key terms of Catholicism. Hardon has also written a larger, more complete Catholic dictionary.

Howard, Thomas. *Evangelical is Not Enough.* San Francisco: Ignatius Press, 1984. Thomas Howard was professor of English at Gordon College in Boston. He converted to Catholicism in 1985; two days later he resigned his faculty position. This book is the story of Howard's pilgrimage from evangelicalism to liturgical Christianity to Roman Catholicism.

Jenkins, Philip. *The New Anti-Catholicism: The Last Acceptable Prejudice.* New York: Oxford Press, 2003. Anti-Catholicism, once thought to be dead, is alive again in the United States, though few people seem to notice or care. In the words of William Donohue, president of the Catholic League for Religious and Civil Rights, "There are few scholars in the nation better equipped to address the subject of anti-Catholicism than Philip Jenkins. That he has succeeded is indisputable. *The New Anti-Catholicism* is thorough, erudite and convincing."

_____. *The Next Christendom: The Coming of Global Christianity.* Oxford: Oxford University Press, 2004. Jenkins charts the rise of global Christianity and predicts the future power shifts within the Christian Church. According to Notre Dame scholar Fr. Virgilio Elizondo, "Like the voice of a sentinel sounding the alert, this book is a fascinating, provocative revelation of the non-Western global Christianity emerging out of Africa, Asia and Latin America."

Karl Keating. *Catholicism and Fundamentalism: The Attack on Romanism by Bible Christians.* San Francisco: Ignatius Press, 1988. A clear, scripturally-based defense of Catholicism from fundamentalist attacks. In the words of Jesuit scholar John A. Hardon, the book is, "A masterpiece of Catholic apologetics. Keating gives a solid defense of Catholicism against the critical attacks of fundamentalists, done with patient clarity that is bound to convince even the most prejudiced critic of Roman Catholicism."

_____. *What Catholics Really Believe: 52 Answers to Common Misconceptions About the Catholic Faith.* San Francisco: Ignatius Press, 1992. Keating discusses fifty-two confusions about the Catholic faith, held by both Catholics and non-Catholics. According to Boston College professor Peter Kreeft, "Keating is one of the best Catholic apologists alive. He writes in the tradition of, and as a worthy successor to, Frank Sheed and Archbishop Fulton Sheen. He is thoroughly orthodox, reasonable, clear and interesting."

Klug, Eugene F. A. *Lift High the Cross: The Theology of Martin Luther.* St. Louis: Concordia Publishing House, 2003. Brief highlights of the life of Martin Luther, interwoven with a summary of his principal written works. A good overview and sampling of Luther's watershed writings.

———————— A Guide to Further Reading ————————

Kreeft, Peter J. *Catholic Christianity*. San Francisco: Ignatius Press, 2001. A complete compendium of all the major beliefs of Catholicism based on the most recent edition of the *Catechism of the Catholic Church*. In the words of Karl Keating, "In *Catholic Christianity*, Peter Kreeft has taken the core of the *Catechism's* teaching and has presented it in his pithy and winning style. The result is the best entrée to the Catechism [and] to the Catholic faith."

Küng, Hans. *The Catholic Church: A Short History*. New York: Random House, 2001. A history of the Catholic Church by one of Catholicism's most controversial scholars and critics.

Lane, Anthony N.S. *Justification by Faith in Catholic-Protestant Dialogue: An Evangelical Assessment*. Edinburgh: T & T Clark, 2002. The doctrine of justification by faith as taught by John Calvin and the Council of Trent. According to evangelical scholar Timothy George, this book is, "A major contribution to a fuller understanding of the article by which the church stands or falls—but, let us pray, may not forever divide."

Longenecker, Dwight. *More Christianity*. Huntington, IN: Our Sunday Visitor, 2002. This book goes beyond C. S. Lewis's *Mere Christianity* to present and explain often contested Catholic doctrines. In the words of Thomas Howard, "We find here all of the questions that arise vis-à-vis the doctrine of the Church ... A beautiful book [that] any believer serious about the ancient faith ought to find justly rewarding."

Longenecker, Dwight, and Gustafson, David. *Mary: A Catholic-Evangelical Debate*. Grand Rapids, MI: Brazos Press, 2003. A lively debate between two graduates of Bob Jones University about the 'Mother of God.' According to Peter Kreeft, "There is simply no other book in print that explores this most immovable impasse [Mary] between Protestants and Catholics in a way that both uncompromising evangelicals and uncompromising

Catholics can wholly applaud. Clear, honest, mutually respectful and illuminating."

Longenecker, Dwight, and Martin, John. *Challenging Catholics: A Catholic-Evangelical Dialogue.* Carlisle, UK: Paternoster Press, 2001. A dialogue between Dwight Longenecker and John Martin, the Australian son of Presbyterian and Brethren parents who is now an Anglican. A wonderful, spirited, well written series of exchanges concerning issues about which Protestants and Catholics disagree. Excellent for those who want to hear both sides of the arguments.

Madrid, Patrick. *Where is That in the Bible?* Huntingdon, IN: Our Sunday Visitor, 2001. A handy reference book with easy-to-use page markings that give scriptural references and support for Catholic beliefs.

Marty, Martin. *Martin Luther.* New York: Penguin Group, 2004. In the words of the publisher, "This [book by Martin Marty, the most influential interpreter of religion in America] is a portrait of a man of consciousness and courage who risked death to witness to his beliefs and whose arguments created changes that altered the destiny of Christendom, the shape of Christianity and the rise of new freedoms in church and state."

Mathison, Keith A. *The Shape of Sola Scriptura.* Moscow, ID: Canon Press, 2001. *Sola scriptura* as understood by evangelicals, Roman Catholics and the Eastern Orthodox. R. C. Sproul, president of Ligonier Ministries, says, "This work is the finest and most comprehensive treatment [of *sola scriptura*] that I have seen."

McCarthy, James G. *The Gospel According to Rome: Comparing Catholic Tradition and the Word of God.* Eugene, OR: Harvest House Publishers, 1995. Former Roman Catholic James McCarthy, the founder and director of Good News for Catholics, Inc., critiques Catholic teachings on justification and salvation, the body and blood of Christ in the Eucharist, various Marian beliefs and the authority of Rome, comparing, in each instance, the *Catechism of the Catholic Church* with scripture. (See below the book that McCarthy coauthored with Catholic priest John Waiss that explores Catholic-Protestant issues in dialogue format.)

McGrath, Alister E. *Reformation Thought: An Introduction*, third edition. Oxford: Blackwell Publishers, 1999. A popular introductory guide for students seeking to understand the central ideas of the European Reformation. Oxford scholar John Platt calls the book, "Vigorous, brisk and highly stimulating. The reader will be thoroughly engaged from the outset, and considerably enlightened at the end."

Noll, Mark A. *Turning Points: Decisive Moments in the History of Christianity*, second edition. Grand Rapids, MI: Baker Book House, 2000. A popular introduction to church history, with sections on the outward movement of the church and the East-West and North-South schisms. *Publishers Weekly* says, "Noll's treatment of the material is evenhanded, engaging and illuminating. This will be a useful text for readers seeking a historical framework within which to understand their Christian faith."

Noll, Mark A., and Nystron, Carolyn. *Is the Reformation Over?: An Evangelical Assessment of Contemporary Roman Catholicism*. Grand Rapids, MI: Baker Book House, 2005. According to Calvin College professor of history Joel Carpenter, "Things are not the way they used to be between evangelicals and Catholics, and Noll and Nystrom show us why, citing the Second Vatican Council's reforms, the charismatic movement, worldwide church growth and renewal, decades of theological dialogue, and a common opposition to secular relativism. The authors are careful to point out both the convergences and the continuing disagreements in doctrine, church order and witness."

O'Collins, Gerald, and Farrugia, Mario. *Catholicism: The Story of Catholic Christianity*. Oxford: Oxford University Press, 2003.

Fathers O'Collins and Farraugia, professors of systematic theology at Gregorian University, provide a lively, readable account of what is distinctively Catholic, while remaining sensitive to other Christians and other religions. In the opinion of Archbishop of Canterbury Rowan Williams, "[This book] can be read with profit and delight as a testament to the great central truths and themes of historic Christianity. A superb achievement."

O'Gorman, Bob, and Faulkner, Mary. *The Complete Idiot's Guide to Understanding Catholicism*. Indianapolis, IN: Alpha Books, 2000. A quick, easy guide to the origins, rise to power and present-day role of the Catholic Church. In the opinion of Martin E. Marty, professor emeritus, University of Chicago, "This book rescues and re-elevates the term *idiot* (from a Greek word that means a lay man or woman who is not a professional or specialist) so that it is no longer an insult. In fact, it applies to most of us, since we are not professionals or specialists in Catholic life and thought."

Oden, Thomas G. *The Justification Reader*. Grand Rapids, MI: Eerdmans Publishing, 2002. A scholarly look at the doctrine of justification by faith by one of America's leading Protestant theologians. According to Christian apologist and author Norman Geisler, "This is a landmark work on a kingpin doctrine by a first-rate scholar who has made a commendable effort to demonstrate doctrinal unity within ecclesiastic plurality."

Pearce, Joseph. *C. S. Lewis and the Catholic Church*. San Francisco: Ignatius Press, 2003. Biographer Joseph Pearce delves into C. S. Lewis's relationship with Catholic friends J.R.R. Tolkien and others, and with the Roman Catholic Church, which he never joined. Author James Como says, "Joseph Pearce has tackled the great Unasked Question and has produced an answer with both muscle and heart. [This book] is a banquet of arguments so provocative, important and inviting that the master himself would find it irresistible."

———————— A Guide to Further Reading ————————

Rausch, Thomas P., S.J., editor. *Catholics and Evangelicals: Do They Share a Common Future?* New York: Paulist Press, 2000. Essays by Catholics and evangelicals about views they share, where they differ and how they might engage in a common mission in today's post-Christian, postmodern society. In the words of Fuller Theological Seminary president Richard J. Mouw, "This book is an important gift to both Catholics and evangelical Protestants. [Here] are serious—and I think quite successful—efforts to get past the long-standing pattern of talking past one another."

Schreck, Alan. *Catholic and Christian: An Explanation of Commonly Misunderstood Catholic Beliefs.* Ann Arbor, MI: Servant Publications, 1984. A concise, readable summary of beliefs which puzzle both Catholics and non-Catholics. Catholic theologian Ralph Martin says, "Christians need to stand together for the gospel. This book fills a much-needed service in shedding light on misunderstood Catholic beliefs."

_____. *The Essential Catholic Catechism.* Ann Arbor, MI: Servant Publications, 1999. A useful resource for anyone interested in learning more about the basic tenets of the Catholic faith. In the words of Cardinal Christoph Schonbörn, "*The Essential Catholic Catechism* presents the Catholic faith for people of today. It is written in everyday language that makes it easy and agreeable to read."

Schwarz, John E. *A Handbook of the Christian Faith.* Minneapolis: Bethany House Publishers, 2004. An overview of the Bible, the person and work of Jesus, the history of the church, Christian beliefs and doctrines, other world religions and belief systems, and how to grow in and live out the Christian faith. According to Luther Seminary professor of theology Patrick Keifert, "This book contains an encyclopedic breadth of information and insights, and materials not usually found in overviews and surveys of the Bible, with an easy-to-read style. I can think of no other introduction, intended for the lay reader, that does the job as well."

Shea, Mark P. *By What Authority?: An Evangelical Discovers Catholic Tradition.* Huntington, IN: Servant Publications, 1996. The journey of a Protestant evangelical to Catholicism and to the belief in 'tradition' as the only sure guarantee of the truth of the revelation of Jesus Christ. Author, apologist and professor of theology Scott Hahn says, "The thing I like most about this book is the crystal clear and compelling case that Shea makes, on the basis of logic, history and scripture, for Sacred ('big T') Tradition."

Tomlin, Graham. *Luther and His World.* Downers Grove, IL: InterVarsity Press, 2002. A wonderful, readable book on the forces and influences that shaped Martin Luther's theology and his emergence as the leading figure of the Reformation. "The person revealed here is by turns obstinate, sensitive, blunt and determined—and a man of faith willing to risk all for his convictions."

Waiss, Fr. John R., and McCarthy, James G. *Letters Between a Catholic and an Evangelical: From Debate to Dialogue on the Issues That Separate Us.* Eugene, OR: Harvest House Publishers, 2003. Father John Waiss, a Catholic priest who serves as a chaplain at Opus Dei centers in California, and Jim McCarthy, a Roman Catholic-turned-evangelical, discuss scripture alone versus scripture and tradition, the teaching authority of the church, the means and assurance of salvation, the sacrament of Eucharist, and the roles of Mary, angels and the saints.

Weigel, George. *The Truth of Catholicism.* New York: HarperCollins Publishers, 1999. George Weigel, one of the world's preeminent commentators on the Catholic Church, explores questions and controversies surrounding Catholicism to bring the truths of Catholicism into clearer focus. According to *Publishers Weekly,* this book, is "An excellent resource for anyone curious enough about Catholicism to look behind the headlines."

White, James R. *The Roman Catholic Controversy.* Minneapolis: Bethany House Publishers, 1996. An absorbing look at current views of scripture, tradition, the papacy, Marian doctrines and other Catholic beliefs. In the opinion of Michael Horton, president of Christians United for Reformation, "[This book] presents an enormous amount of primary-source research that is balanced with a sense of proportion often lacking in similar critiques."

Index of Names

Albrecht, Archbishop (1490–1545), 19
Althus, Paul (1888–1966), 2
Ambrose, Bishop (c. 339–397), 2, 52, 97
Antiochus Epiphanes (d. 164), 112
Aquinas, Thomas (1225–1274), 10, 52
Athenagoras I, Patriarch (1886–1972), 12
Augustine, Saint (354–430), 8, 48, 52, 97, 111

Barth, Karl (1886–1968), 39
Benedict, Saint (480–550), 10
Benedict XVI, Pope (b. 1927), 122
Bokenkotter, Thomas, 26
Boleyn, Anne (1507–1536), 25
Bonhoeffer, Dietrich (1906–1945), 60
Buechner, Frederick (b. 1926), 2

Calvin, John (1509–1564), 21, 23, 24, 25

Catherine of Aragon (1485–1536), 24
Cerularius, Michael (d. 1058), 12
Charlemange (c. 742–814), 9
Charles V, Emperor (1500–1558), 20, 23, 24
Chesterton, G. K. (1874–1936), 36
Clement of Rome (c. 100), 51, 69
Clement VII, Pope (1478–1534), 24, 69
Colson, Charles (b. 1931), 119
Columbus, Christopher (1451–1506), 27
Constantine, Emperor (280–337), 7, 9, 10
Cranmer, Thomas (1489–1556), 23, 24

Damacus, Pope (c. 304–384), 111
Dominic, Saint (1170–1221), 10, 108
Duns Scotus, John (1266–1308), 52, 74

Eck, Johannes (1486-1543), 47
Edward VI, King (1537-1553), 25
Elizabeth I, Queen (1533-1603), 25
Erasmus (1466-1536), 20

Ferdinand, King (1452-1516), 16, 24
Fox, George (1624-1691), 26
Francis of Assisi (1182-1226), 10
Frederick the Wise (1463-1525), 20

Geisler, Norman, 89
Gibson, David, 94
Godfrey, Robert, 47
Gregory I, Pope (540-604), 9, 52
Gregory IX, Pope (1170-1241), 116

Henry VIII, King (1491-1547), 17, 24-25
Hill, Kent, 119
Horton, Walter, 119

Ignatius of Antioch (35-117), 10, 66
Ignatius of Loyola (1491-1556), 66
Irenaeus (130-202), 51, 69
Isabella, Queen (1451-1504), 16, 24

Jenkins, Philip (b. 1952), 101
Jerome, Saint (340-420), 20, 51, 76, 111, 113
John of Damascus (c. 675-749), 52, 79, 80
John XXIII, Pope (1881-1963), 81, 122
John Paul II, Pope (1920-2005), 81
Judas Maccabeus (d. 160 BC), 112

Julius III, Pope (1487-1555), 9
Kierkegaard, Søren (1813-1855), 34
Knox, John (1514-1572), 23
Kreeft, Peter (b. 1938), 35, 87, 113

Leo I, Pope (d. 461), 9, 52
Leo III, Pope (d. 816), 9
Leo IX, Pope (1002-1054), 12
Leo X, Pope (1475-1521), 19
Lewis, C. S. (1898-1963), 30
Little, Paul (1928-1975), 2
Luther, Martin (1483-1546), 8, 18-21, 23, 24, 25, 47, 60, 100, 112, 117

MacKenzie, Ralph, 89
Mary Tudor (1516-1558), 24, 25
Mathison, Keith, 64
McCarthy, James G., 55
Melanchthon, Philip (1497-1560), 23
Menninger, Karl (1893-1990), 36
Menno Simons (1496-1561), 25

Neuhaus, Richard John (b. 1950), 119
Newman, John Henry (1801-1890), 53

O'Connor, D. W., 65

Packer, J. I. (b. 1926), 119
Paul VI, Pope (1897-1978), 12, 54, 67, 81
Peter Lombard (1095-1169), 52, 104

Index of Names

Pius IX, Pope (1792-1878), 53, 54, 74
Pius XII, Pope (1876-1958), 53, 54, 63, 79
Polycarp (69-155), 69

Ratzinger, Joseph (b. 1927), 64
Robeck, Cecil, 39
Robinson, John A. T. (1919-1983), 5

Schillebeeckx, Edward (b. 1914), 83
Seymore, Jane (1509-1537), 25
Sixtus IV, Pope (1414-1484), 16
Smyth, John (1554-1612), 26

Teresa, Mother (1910-1997), 116
Tertullian, Quintus (160-220), 48, 64, 69, 83

Urban VIII, Pope (1568-1644), 9

von Bora, Katharina (1499-1552), 20

Ward, Keith, 38
Ware, Bishop Kallistos, 3
Weigel, George, 119, 120
Wesley, Charles (1707-1788), 26, 78
Wesley, John (1703-1791), 26, 78
William of Ockham (1285-1349), 52
Wills, Garry, 98
Wycliffe, John (1329-1384), 18

Zwingli, Ulrich (1484-1531), 23

About the Authors

John Schwarz is a lawyer and CPA who spent his working life in the corporate business world. In 1984, when the last of their children went off to college, John retired and he and his wife went to Kenya as missionaries. John taught accounting in a Christian liberal arts college; he and his wife started a community-based health care program on the outskirts of Nairobi; and they started and ran for several years a primary school in a large slum in Nairobi. In between trips back and forth to Africa, John went to Regent College, a graduate school of theology in Vancouver, British Columbia, where he earned a Masters of Christian Studies degree.

When John and his wife returned to Minneapolis, John began producing videos for in-church adult education programs and small groups. The video presenters in the series included, among others, John Stott, Martin Marty, Tony Campolo, N. T. (Tom) Wright, John Ortberg and Raymond Bakke. John also wrote a book on Christianity, called *A Handbook of the Christian Faith*, published by Bethany House Publishers, which has been translated into French, Spanish, Portuguese, Hindi and other languages.

John was raised and confirmed in the Episcopal Church, which he refers to several times in the text. When their children were growing up, John and his wife attended a Congregational Church; when they lived in Nairobi, they attended an indigenous Baptist church; when they lived in Vancouver, they attended a Plymouth Brethren chapel. Today John and his wife worship in an inner-city Methodist church in Minneapolis in the summer and a Covenant church in Scottsdale in the winter.

Dwight Longenecker is an American who has lived in England for more than twenty years. He holds degrees in English/Speech from Bob Jones University and a degree in theology from Oxford University. A former Anglican priest and now a Catholic, Dwight writes regularly for more than twenty magazines, newspapers and journals in Great Britain and the United States.

Dwight has authored eight books on religion and spirituality. His first book, *The Path to Rome—Modern Journeys to the Catholic Faith*, was published by Gracewing in 1999; it has been reprinted every year since its publication. *Listen My Son* (Gracewing/Morehouse, 2000) is a daily devotional which applies The Rule of Saint Benedict to the task of modern parenting. *Challenging Catholics* (Paternoster, 2001) was written with John Martin, the former editor of the Church of England newspaper. The book is a hard-hitting dialogue based on the two authors' Premier Radio series by the same name. *St. Benedict and St. Thérèse* (Gracewing/Our Sunday Visitor, 2002) is a study of the lives of two of Catholicism's most popular saints. *More Christianity* (Our Sunday Visitor, 2002) is a popular-level argument for Catholicism as the fullest expression of the Christian faith. *Mary—A Catholic-Evangelical Debate* (Brazos Press, 2003) is a dialogue between Dwight and David Gustafson, an evangelical Protestant, on the role and importance of the Blessed Virgin Mary. *Adventures in Orthodoxy* (Sophia, 2003) is a Chestertonian romp through the Apostles' Creed. *Christianity Pure & Simple* (Catholic Truth Society, 2003) is a series of five booklets that explain the Catholic faith in down-to-earth language for ordinary people.

Dwight is also the Creative Director of a consultancy and training company called Working Hero, and the founder of the charity Ordinary Hero. Both the charity and the business use plot lines and characters from stories to help companies and individuals go on adventures of positive change.